ENDORSEMENTS FOR

MW00563469

Sharla Fritz has done it again! Her new Bible study, *Measured by Grace*, will challenge you to look at the way you view success and see if your vision is that of the world or of God. Sharla has done all of the research for you! She is meticulous about details and gives you the background story, timelines, maps, and Scripture verses you need. You will learn about eight people and places from the Bible that will let you know that though we all have weaknesses like they did, God loves us and can use us for His mission to save souls for His glory. You will enjoy your journey through this wonderful Bible study!

—Susan Bell, president of LWML Eastern District,
2018–2022

Sharla Fritz offers a gracious gift in her new study, *Measured by Grace*, to all those who feel moored down by their mistakes and mess-ups. We are reminded over and over again through this study of God's Word that our failures do not have the final say over our lives. God steps into our brokenness and redeems our stories. What a comfort to know that our lives are transformed by God's grace.

—Michelle Diercks, author of *Promised Rest:
Finding Peace in God's Presence*

Sharla has carefully done an amazing amount of research that will make biblical characters we already know and love come alive even more as we dig deeper into their stories. Sharla walks the reader through understanding the not-so-pretty sides of these people while also pointing us to God's grace, love, and forgiveness. God can use our faults in spite of ourselves and draw people closer to Him through the process. Though we fail God, He never fails us. In fact, He uses us in the midst of our failures. To Him be the glory!

—Molly Dixon, online Bible study leader

Sharla's writing in *Measured by Grace* is a prism. Through her thorough and varied perspectives, she highlights God's love and grace in Scripture and through the stories of His people. I love the deep dive she does into our concept of success and her beautiful encouragement that we are measured by grace.

—Christina Hergenrader, author of *Inspired by the Holy
Spirit: Four Habits for Faithful Living*

In *Measured by Grace: How God Defines Success*, Sharla Fritz thoughtfully examines the biblical stories of eight far-from-perfect men and women. Like us, their lives overflowed with blunders, failures, struggles, and sin. But, remarkably, God stuck with them, nurtured them, forgave them, and even helped them to do His good work. What an encouraging reminder for us! This book, full of humor and history and wisdom, stands alone as a good read about success in God's eyes. But Sharla's addition of clear and succinct study questions also makes this a fabulous book to read and discuss in a group setting.

—Afton Rorvik, author of *Living Connected:
An Introvert's Guide to Friendship*

MEASURED BY GRACE

HOW GOD DEFINES SUCCESS

SHARLA FRITZ

CONCORDIA PUBLISHING HOUSE • SAINT LOUIS

DEDICATION

To John, who has made our life together a stupendous success.

Published by Concordia Publishing House
3558 S. Jefferson Ave., St. Louis, MO 63118-3968
1-800-325-3040 • cph.org

Unless otherwise indicated, Scripture quotations are from the ESV® Bible (The Holy
Bible, English Standard Version®), copyright © 2001 by Crossway, a publishing ministry of Good News Publishers. Used by permission. All rights reserved.

Scripture quotation taken from the Amplified® Bible (AMP), copyright © 2015 by The
Lockman Foundation. Used by permission. www.lockman.org

Quotations from *The Lutheran Study Bible*, copyright © 2009 Concordia Publishing
House. All rights reserved.

Quotations from *Luther's Small Catechism with Explanation*, copyright © 1986, 2017
Concordia Publishing House. All rights reserved.

Quotation marked *LSB* is from *Lutheran Service Book*, copyright © 2006 Concordia
Publishing House. All rights reserved.

Manufactured in the United States of America

1 2 3 4 5 6 7 8 9 10   31 30 29 28 27 26 25 24 23 22

CONTENTS

INTRODUCTION

Stage lights illuminated my hands as my fingers flew through Schumann's *Papillons*. I had practiced for months leading up to this important piano recital. But suddenly, my preparation failed me. I couldn't remember what came next! Before anyone noticed (I hoped), I jumped back to a place in the music I was sure of. But when I reached the sticking point, again I couldn't go on. I repeated this loop several times before I could finally finish the piece. The applause at the end couldn't drown out the voice in my head: *You should have done better.*

My sister-in-law led the way down Big Mountain in Montana on our last run of the day, her skis easily gliding over the snow. I, however, looked far less elegant, as this was only my third attempt at downhill skiing and my legs felt like Jell-O. Tired and cold, I kept falling, picking myself up out of the snow, and falling again. When a ski patrol guy joined us, I told him, "You can go ahead. I'm just taking my time." But he said it was his job to make sure everyone made it off the mountain safely. As I took another face-plant in the cold white stuff, I thought, *Great! Now I can be tired, cold, and mortified.*

The hurt look on my husband's face said it all. Hurtful words had escaped my lips, and now I witnessed the damage done. Why had I said that? Why couldn't I think before I spoke? Only this morning I had prayed that the Holy Spirit would guide my speech, yet again unkind words had spilled out. Even after we talked things through and my husband reassured me of his forgiveness, I wondered, *Will I ever change?*

What do all of these stories have in common?

Failure.

You might not have flubbed your college piano recital or embarrassed yourself on the ski slope, but you likely have your own stories of regrets and mistakes. We've all messed up. We've all come up short. We've all blown it.

And our blunders, our shortcomings, our sins haunt us. In our success-worshiping society, our failures make us feel worthless. After all, our culture applauds the athlete who wins the gold medal, the actor who receives the Oscar, the businessperson who climbs to the top of the corporate ladder. It ignores the runner who came in last, the actress with the bit part, the employee in the mail room. If our names aren't on the plaque, do we matter? Sometimes we might even wonder if God can bring anything good out of our mistake-riddled attempts and see past our mediocre existences.

God's Word tells us that He loves us despite our failings and imperfections. To reassure us, the Lord shares stories of flawed people in His Word. *Measured by Grace* will give you a peek into the lives of eight of those people. Joseph needed to experience a metaphorical face-plant before he rose to the second-highest position in Egypt. Rahab had a not-so-pristine past. David was a supersize sinner. Jeremiah looked like a professional failure. John the Baptist lived the life of a social misfit. The woman at the well had messed up repeatedly. Peter had one critical moment of disloyalty. And Paul? He described himself as the worst sinner of all.

When you study these stories, you will discover that God's measuring stick is nothing like the world's. Our culture gauges our worth by outward standards of wealth and fame, but the Lord uses criteria like humility and faithfulness. So although most of the people we will study would have been pronounced a failure by the world, God deemed their lives a success.

Why would God include these stories of mess-ups and mistakes? Because they show us the power of His transformative grace. No blunder is too big for His benevolence. No gaffe too huge for His goodness. No slipup too large for His saving power. God can take all of our missteps and make them into miracles.

Read on and see that God's definition of success is nothing like the world's. Witness how He redeems failure for His glory. Learn how the Lord doesn't give up on those the world labels also-rans, might-have-beens, and good-for-nothings. Experience the freedom of being measured by grace.

Using This Book

In *Measured by Grace*, you will spend time getting to know eight people in the Bible who either experienced a big failure or didn't look successful in the eyes of the world. You'll learn more about their lives and their times in history. You'll discover how God transformed their failure or insignificance. You will examine their ancient stories in Scripture and glean lessons for your life right now.

You may choose to study the concepts of failure and success by reading straight through the chapters. The readings include

- **a timeline** to help you see how that particular Bible character's life fits in history;
- **a map** to give geographical perspective of where he or she lived; and
- **historical information** about the time and place to help you envision how each Bible character lived.

In addition to reading the chapters, I hope you will take time to go deeper into the Word by engaging in the Bible study questions (beginning on page 143). This section includes

- **Reflect on the Reading:** questions about the chapter;
- **Dig into the Word:** questions to help you go deeper into the biblical accounts;
- **Apply the Word to Your Life:** ways to use the lessons in your ordinary days; and
- **Create a Project:** hands-on activities to help you remember what you've learned, plus a playlist of music to uplift your heart

I invite you to gather a few others to join you as you examine these stories of success and failure. Share your own stories and encourage one another. The study is designed to be completed in eight weeks, but if your meeting time is short or you simply want to take the journey a little more slowly, you may choose to take two weeks for every chapter. In that case, you could do the reading and the "Reflect on the Reading" questions the first week and the "Dig into Scripture," "Apply the Word to Your Life," and "Create a Project" sections the next week. The "Create a Project" activities may be especially enjoyable to complete as a group. In fact, you might want to have the materials for the activity set out for participants to work on as they arrive for the study. You could also have the suggested songs playing in the background—tuning the hearts of everyone to God's love.

As you study,

- begin with prayer;
- rely on Scripture to guide your discussions; and
- keep what is shared confidential unless you are given permission to share outside the group.

May the Lord bless you as you rejoice in God's power to transform failure into faith.

CHAPTER 1

JOSEPH: DETOURED DREAMER

TIMELINE

Joseph .... 1915 BC

One pathetic ray of sunlight pushed its way through the high windows in the mud-brick wall. Joseph dragged his weary body across the room and sat on the dirt floor in the tiny pool of light—an act of hope in this dark and depressing place. Months had passed since his fellow prisoner had been reinstated to his position as official taste tester for Pharaoh. Joseph remembered the cupbearer's excitement when he had interpreted the man's dream about branches and grapes and had said he would get out of prison and regain his position.

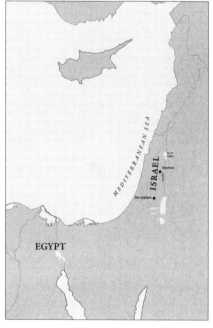

Map © iStock / Peter Hermes Furian

Joseph implored the cupbearer to remember him and mention him to Pharaoh. "Please," he pleaded, "help me. I haven't done anything to earn a place in this pit."

But that had been almost a year ago, and Joseph now wondered if he would ever see the light of day again. It seemed his life continued in a downward trajectory of one disappointment after another.

It had all started out so promising. Life with eleven brothers had its challenges, but he knew he had his father's love even if he didn't have theirs.

Joseph thought back to his dreams; he still recalled them clearly. The first one took place in the fields. He and his brothers were binding sheaves of grain. His stood upright, but his brothers' sheaves encircled his and bent down to it. In the second dream, the sun, moon, and eleven stars bowed to him. He didn't fully understand those dreams—and he probably shouldn't have mentioned them to his brothers—but somehow the dreams made him feel that God had an important role for him.

Now he was doubtful. His interpretations of the cupbearer's and baker's dreams had come true, but it looked like he had misunderstood his own. Instead of rising to a significant position, he sat on the floor of a dark prison. Instead of success, he experienced nothing but failure.

> ### KEY VERSE
> The LORD was with Joseph, and he became a successful man. (Genesis 39:2)

How does our culture measure success? It certainly looks like the world's success meter rises with every dollar earned, promotion granted, or trophy won, and plummets with each financial loss, professional downfall, or athletic defeat.

Joseph's life included both extremes of devastating loss and amazing achievement. Yet a close study of his story reveals God's surprising definition of success.

Setting the Scene

Joseph's story begins around 1915 BC. Born to the patriarch Jacob (also known as Israel) and his favorite wife, Rachel, Joseph lived with them in a home that likely bustled with the activity of a large family—two wives, two concubines, twelve sons, and one daughter. Jacob had started his family in Haran where he tended sheep for his uncle Laban, but shortly after Joseph was born, Jacob left Haran and moved back to his homeland of Canaan. On the journey back, Joseph's mother went into labor with her second child, Benjamin, and died giving birth.

Scripture tells us, "Now Israel loved Joseph more than any other of his sons, because he was the son of his old age" (Genesis 37:3). And he didn't hide his favoritism. Instead, he demonstrated Joseph's status by making him a special—maybe even "technicolor"—robe. This coat made Jacob's favoritism incredibly obvious, and the other brothers began to resent Joseph.

Joseph didn't make it any easier for them to like him when he told them about his dreams. When they heard about sheaves of grain and eleven stars bowing down to their arrogant little brother, they hated him even more and plotted to kill him. But then they had a better idea and sold him to a passing caravan of Ishmaelites on their way to Egypt.

I wonder what went through Joseph's head as he trekked to Egypt. Certainly those dreams came back to him time and again, and maybe he laughed at the irony. The dreams gave him visions of becoming someone special. Now he was tied to a camel, dragged to a far-off land where he definitely would not wear a special coat or receive any favoritism.

Success in Egypt

When the caravan arrived in Egypt, the Ishmaelites sold Joseph to Potiphar, an officer of Pharaoh and captain of the guard. Joseph became a house slave, but it didn't take long for Potiphar to notice the quality of Joseph's work. Joseph advanced to the position of Potiphar's personal attendant (Genesis 39:4) and then to overseer of everything in his master's house (v. 5). Potiphar noticed that "the LORD caused all that he did to succeed in his hands" (v. 3).

Things were looking up for Joseph, but there was just one problem. Potiphar's wife had her eye on handsome Joseph. Day after day, she tried to entice him into her bed. Day after day, he turned her down.

But one day when no one else was in the house, Potiphar's wife grabbed Joseph's clothes and tried again. "Lie with me," she said (v. 12). Joseph ran off in such a hurry that he left his garment in her hand, and the rejected woman used it as evidence that Joseph had tried to seduce her. She told her husband, "The Hebrew servant, whom you have brought among us, came in to me to laugh at me. But as soon as I lifted up my voice and cried, he left his garment beside me and fled out of the house" (vv. 17–18).

The Bible says Potiphar's "anger was kindled" (v. 19), but commentators wonder if he directed the anger toward his wife more than Joseph. If Potiphar believed Joseph had sexually assaulted his wife, he would have ordered Joseph's immediate execution. Jails were not common in ancient Egypt. They only held political prisoners while they waited for a trial or execution.[1] Also, it appears that this prison was under Potiphar's direction and even on the premises of his home. Genesis 40:3 tells us the cupbearer and chief baker were put "in custody in the house of the captain of the guard, in the prison where Joseph was confined." Still, prison was prison, and ancient jails were not known for pampering inmates.

Yet again, Joseph shows his stuff, and not much time passes before the keeper of the prison notices the young Hebrew and puts him in charge of all the other prisoners. Even in this lowest place, Joseph shone. "Whatever he did, the LORD made it succeed" (Genesis 39:23).

IS THIS SUCCESS?

I wonder: Did it feel like success to Joseph? Before prison, the work he did for Potiphar made the Egyptian's home thrive. His master noticed Joseph's excellent efforts and gave him more and more responsibility, until "he left all that he had in Joseph's charge" (Genesis 39:6). The jailer, too,

JOSEPH'S CLOTHES

If you know me, you know I like clothes! My closet bulges with too many pants, tops, and sweaters. My love of clothes made me notice that clothing is a significant theme in Joseph's story.

We all know about the fancy robe Jacob gave Joseph—if only from the Broadway musical *Joseph and the Amazing Technicolor Dreamcoat*. Perhaps you remember Sunday School lessons or flannelgraph figures of Joseph wearing a coat with colorful stripes. Actually, we don't know what that famous coat looked like because the Hebrew word used to describe it appears only twice: in Joseph's story and in 2 Samuel regarding Tamar's garment (2 Samuel 13:19). Most commentators agree that the coat Jacob made for his favorite son was a full-length coat with long sleeves—a coat that would have indicated superior rank.[2] Paintings from this period give more clues. Canaanite travelers in some Egyptian paintings are dressed in long embroidered garments with long fringed scarves wrapped around their bodies.[3]

We don't know what Joseph's coat looked like, but his brothers knew what it meant: their father loved *him* more. And without that coat, Joseph was a nobody—even less than a nobody: a slave on his way to Egypt.

In Egypt, Joseph's clothing was again used against him. When Potiphar's wife unsuccessfully tried to seduce Joseph, she grabbed his garment as he ran from her grasp. She claimed that the cloak proved Joseph's attempted assault.

Finally, when Pharaoh elevated Joseph to second-in-command, he gave Joseph fine garments of linen, plus some serious bling—an official signet ring and a gold chain for his neck. Although Joseph's clothing had brought him trouble in the past, it now announced his important position.

> The Bible often uses the symbolism of clothing to describe our spiritual condition. Isaiah pronounces our sinful state as "unclean" and says "our righteous deeds are like a polluted garment" (Isaiah 64:6). But God washes those garments "whiter than snow" (Psalm 51:7) and, because of Christ, He clothes us in "garments of salvation" and covers us with "the robe of righteousness" (Isaiah 61:10).

EVERYTHING JOSEPH DID TURNED TO GOLD—FOR SOMEONE ELSE.

noticed Joseph's excellent management skills and put him in charge of the prisoners. (This in itself is remarkable. Who would put one inmate in charge of others?) Even one of the other prisoners benefited from Joseph's unique abilities. Joseph's interpretation of the cupbearer's dream came true and this servant of Pharaoh was released from jail. Everything Joseph did turned to gold—for someone else.

If someone had said to Joseph, "The LORD was with Joseph, and he became a successful man" (Genesis 39:2), he might have laughed out loud. Scripture tells us Joseph was seventeen years old when his brothers sold him into slavery (Genesis 37:2) and thirty years old when Pharaoh made him second-in-command (Genesis 41:46). Joseph spent thirteen years as a slave and a prisoner. I doubt he would have described himself as successful.

Nor would we use the word *successful* to describe a lowly servant or prisoner. *Successful* is the term we use for champions and award winners. So how do we reconcile the differences? Why does the Bible describe Joseph as successful?

SUCCESS IN JOSEPH'S WORK

To understand, let's examine the three stories of Joseph's work in Egypt. When we study narrative stories in Scripture that are similar, we can better understand their meanings as we look at what the storyteller repeats and what he doesn't.[4]

First, let's look at the account of Joseph in Potiphar's house:

> Now Joseph had been brought down to Egypt, and Potiphar, an officer of Pharaoh, the captain of the guard, an Egyptian, had bought him from the Ishmaelites who had brought him down there. The LORD was with Joseph, and he became a successful man, and he was in the house of his Egyptian master. His master saw that the LORD was with him and that the LORD caused all that he did to succeed in his hands. So Joseph found favor in his sight and attended him, and he made him overseer of his house and put him in charge of all that he had. From the time that he made him overseer in his house and over all that he had, the LORD blessed the Egyptian's house for Joseph's sake; the blessing of the LORD was on all that he had, in house and field. So he left all that he had in Joseph's charge, and because of him he had no concern about anything but the food he ate. (Genesis 39:1–6)

Now compare this narrative with the story of Joseph's time in prison:

> And Joseph's master took him and put him into the prison, the place where the king's prisoners were confined, and he was there in prison. But the LORD was with Joseph and showed him steadfast love and gave him favor in the sight of the keeper of the prison. And the keeper of the prison put Joseph in charge of all the prisoners who were in the prison. Whatever was done there, he was the one who did it. The keeper of the prison paid no attention to anything that was in Joseph's charge, because the LORD was with him. And whatever he did, the LORD made it succeed. (Genesis 39:20–23)

Similar, right? Verses 2 and 21 both tell us that "the LORD was with Joseph." In fact, Joseph's life displayed God's presence so clearly that Potiphar and the jailer both recognized that the Lord was with him (vv. 3, 23). And because they recognized that God's blessings followed Joseph wherever he went, both gave Joseph added responsibility. Potiphar "put him in

DREAMS

Dreams appear as a significant theme in Joseph's story. His dreams of bowing sheaves and genuflecting stars give him a one-way ticket to trouble. His analyses of the cupbearer's and baker's dreams establish his reputation as an interpreter of dreams. Finally, Pharaoh's troubling dreams give Joseph an opportunity to get out of prison, and his interpretations of those dreams then make Joseph's childhood dreams come true.

Dreams held great significance in ancient times. Trained dream experts were sought out for their interpretations. Egyptian and Babylonian interpreters consulted "dream books," which recorded sample dreams and their meanings. Consulting these books gave a "scientific" authenticity to their interpretations.[5]

Instead of dream books, Joseph relied on the wisdom of God. Still, his interpretations mirrored some of the principles from these manuals, such as the number of items in a dream signifying the number of days or years.[6]

Today we must use caution with dreams. God may still communicate through dreams, but we must always check the message against the inerrant Word of God.

charge of all that he had" (v. 4), and because of Joseph's abilities, "he had no concern about anything but the food he ate" (v. 6). The jailer "paid no attention to anything that was in Joseph's charge, because the LORD was with him" (v. 23).

We find similar statements about success. Genesis 39:3 says of Joseph's time with Potiphar, "The LORD caused all that he did to succeed in his hands." And verse 23 tells us about his time in jail: "Whatever he did, the LORD made it succeed." Even if Joseph would not have described himself as successful, the Lord did.

Now let's jump ahead to the account of Joseph's rise to power. Two years after the cupbearer got out of prison, Pharaoh had some troubling dreams (Genesis 41). When no one could interpret them, the royal taste tester suddenly remembered Joseph. Pharaoh sent for Joseph and described the dreams. Joseph explained to the Egyptian ruler that the dreams foretold seven years of plenty followed by seven years of famine. Joseph then suggested a plan for storing grain from the bountiful years so it would be available for the lean years.

This proposal pleased Pharaoh, who said to his servants, "'Can we find a man like this, in whom is the Spirit of God?' Then Pharaoh said to Joseph, 'Since God has shown you all this, there is none so discerning and wise as you are. You shall be over my house, and all my people shall order themselves as you command. Only as regards the throne will I be greater than you'" (Genesis 41:37–40). Joseph now had greater responsibility than ever before.

However, something is missing. Both of the other stories spoke about Joseph's success, but that word doesn't appear here. Joseph had success when he served as a slave and languished in jail, but not when he became the second-most-powerful man in the world? Throughout the account of the famine and Joseph collecting grain and selling it to the people, preventing nationwide starvation, the Bible doesn't include a phrase like "the LORD caused everything Joseph did to succeed."

Perhaps Scripture omits the phrase because Joseph's success is so obvious there's no need to point it out. But remember the principle that says we need to pay attention when the story repeats something in one place and omits it in another? Perhaps the omission of the word *success* when Joseph clearly obtains it demonstrates how God defines that word.

Success in the world looks big—stadiums filled with fans. Success in the world looks impressive—fancy corner offices with diplomas on the walls. Success looks like fame—names on brightly lit marquees.

ALTHOUGH WE MAY VIEW OUR LIVES AS DISAPPOINTMENTS, GOD DECLARES THEM TRIUMPHANT WHEN WE TRUST HIM TO COMPLETE THE WORK HE HAS GIVEN US— GREAT OR SMALL.

But success in God's eyes doesn't necessarily look big or impressive. The Hebrew word for "success" in Genesis 39 is *salah*. It means "to advance, prosper, make progress, succeed, be profitable."[7] The word sometimes portrays worldly success that even evil people can achieve, such as in Psalm 37:7: "Fret not yourself over the one who prospers [*salah*] in his way, over the man who carries out evil devices!" But usually, success in the Old Testament doesn't happen without the Lord's help. We see this in Joseph's story: "The LORD caused all that he did to succeed in his hands" (Genesis 39:3). We also see it in the account of King Uzziah where it says, "As long as he sought the LORD, God made him prosper" (2 Chronicles 26:5).

The success the Bible talks about is not primarily worldly prosperity but submission to the Lord and living in His presence.[8] In Joseph's story, God described Joseph as successful when he was a slave and a prisoner. God measures our success based on our dependence on Him. Although we may view our lives as disappointments, God declares them triumphant when we trust Him to complete the work He has given us—great or small.

SUCCESS IN THE SMALL

I know about small. I have always dreamed of big—but my life has turned out small. I hate to admit this, but when I achieved good grades in school and people told me I would go far, I hoped to make a name for myself. But my life didn't turn out that way. And when people ask about my piano teaching, my writing, or my role in our church, I catch myself apologizing for the lack of greatness. "I love teaching piano, but I only have a few students." "Yes, I've written a few books, but none has ever made a best-seller list." "I play piano for our church services and direct the choir, but we're a very small congregation." Why do I feel the need to make such excuses?

Maybe you have similar phrases to describe yourself: "I'm only a stay-at-home mom." "I'm just a receptionist." "I work behind the scenes as an assistant. No one notices me."

Joseph may have felt the same way. His dreams of sheaves and stars may have given him ideas of greatness. But he was a mere slave. In fact, instead of the achievement freedom would have given, he was relegated to prison.

But God noticed Joseph's faith in Him. Every step of the way, the Lord blessed Joseph's work. Although everyone else would have applauded his achievement when he directed the food supply of a nation, God declared Joseph a success when he scrubbed floors and took meals to prisoners.

WHEN YOU FEEL SMALL

So what can you do when you feel small? when it feels like success has passed you by?

Let's look at some suggestions from Joseph's life.

Do your best in whatever position you find yourself. When Joseph was a slave, he could have moped and complained to God and done his work half-heartedly, but the Bible doesn't tell us that he did so. As a slave, he could not have avoided work, but I doubt Potiphar would have put Joseph in charge of his household if Joseph had made only minimal effort.

WHATEVER WORK YOU FIND YOURSELF DOING—BALANCING THE BOOKS, TEACHING RAMBUNCTIOUS PRE-SCHOOLERS, RUNNING A MULTINATIONAL COR-PORATION, SCRUBBING MUDDY FLOORS—KNOW THAT GOD NOTICES YOUR FAITHFULNESS.

We, too, can do whatever job God has given us to the best of our ability. I can complain about the number of piano students I have, or I can help each student to grow in his or her musical ability. I can hone my writing craft and become a better wordsmith, not to sell more books, but because God has called me to be a writer.

Whatever work you find yourself doing—balancing the books, teaching rambunctious preschoolers, running a multinational corporation, scrubbing muddy floors—know that God notices your vocation. You are doing important work even if the world says it's lowly. Colossians 3:23–24 says, "Whatever you do, work heartily, as for the Lord and not for men, knowing that from the Lord you will receive the inheritance as your reward. You are serving the Lord Christ." Do your best because you serve a God who is gracious to you.

Learn humility and servanthood. The omniscient God knew all along that Joseph would be in charge of feeding the world during a famine. Therefore, although Joseph's brothers intended to kill him, God used them to get Joseph to Egypt where his God-given gifts would be put to use in a crisis.

When we read of how Joseph told his family about his dreams, he comes across as more than a little spoiled. I wish I could hear Joseph's tone of voice when he said, "Hear this dream that I have dreamed: . . . your sheaves gathered around it and bowed down to my sheaf" (Genesis 37:6–7). Did he say it with a good measure of arrogance to flaunt his position over his brothers? Or did his words simply reveal the naivete of a seventeen-year-old unaware of how his dreams would fuel the fire of his brothers' indignation? Either way, Joseph's words demonstrate more than a little self-centeredness.

Our takeaway is that God arranged for Joseph to land in a place where the world did not revolve around him. A place where he would serve instead of being served and bow down instead of being bowed to. Being ordered about as a slave must have been a rude awakening for the spoiled son of Jacob. Joseph learned humility. He learned servanthood.

Even as we work in our small places, we can also learn humility and servanthood. This is the downward journey of all Christian growth—a journey that Christ Himself demonstrated. The apostle Paul instructs, "Have this mind among yourselves, which is yours in Christ Jesus, who, though He was in the form of God, did not count equality with God a thing to be grasped, but emptied Himself, by taking the form of a servant, being born

JOSEPH—A TYPE OF CHRIST

Joseph's life and character are sometimes compared to Jesus'. In fact, commentators describe Joseph as a type of Christ— someone who foreshadows Jesus. Both were sent from their homes for the ultimate purpose of rescuing the world. Both were sold for a few pieces of silver. Both resisted temptation. Both suffered unjustly. Joseph saved a nation from starvation. Jesus saved the world from eternal death.

in the likeness of men" (Philippians 2:5–7). Embracing our small roles as an opportunity to learn service puts us in good company.

Realize real success comes from God. Western culture applauds the self-made man or woman. Our society cheers for the entrepreneur who builds a Fortune 500 company by starting in the garage and the star who skyrockets from humble beginnings to Hollywood fame. But the Bible doesn't talk about success that way.

Even though we can surmise that Joseph worked hard in his lowly positions, Scripture doesn't credit his ingenuity or diligence for the success he experienced. Rather, the Bible says, "the LORD caused all that he did to succeed in his hands" (Genesis 39:3, emphasis added). Without God's blessing, Joseph's labor would not have prospered. He could have been stuck weeding Potiphar's garden for the rest of his life.

Yes, God wants us to put in our best efforts, but the world doesn't always reward humble diligence and thoroughness. I'm sure we've all experienced this. Perhaps you spent many hours starting a business with a fail-safe plan but ended up with nothing to show for it. Or maybe you toiled long days on a project for the company you work for, only to watch someone else get the recognition.

God grants success. And He knows the best for us—whether that's fame and big paychecks or obscurity and a lifestyle that requires us to econo-mize. If God does grant us results that overlap with the kind of success the world notices, let's tell everyone where that success came from. Joseph gave the Lord credit for the success he had in dream interpretation. He told the cupbearer and baker, "Do not interpretations belong to God?" (Genesis 40:8). When Pharaoh asked Joseph about his abilities, Joseph said, "It is not in me; God will give Pharaoh a favorable answer" (Genesis 41:16). Joseph knew God gave him success.

Lean on God's presence and steadfast love. How did Joseph survive thirteen long years in a strange country as a slave and prisoner? The account in Genesis 39 states four times that "the LORD was with him" (vv. 2, 3, 21, 23). We don't know how Joseph knew that the Lord walked beside him in that foreign, polytheistic country, but it is noteworthy that Joseph is the only person in all of Genesis described as having the Spirit of God upon him (Genesis 41:38).[9]

One commentator suggests that Joseph clung to the dreams God had given him as we would grasp onto promises from God's Word. Joseph didn't know how God would make those dreams happen, but he believed God had given them to him and would complete His plans for Joseph's life.[10]

Both the story of Joseph in Potiphar's house and the account of Joseph in prison tell us the Lord was with him, but when Joseph is in prison, the text adds a significant point: "But the LORD was with Joseph and showed him steadfast love" (Genesis 39:21). What grace! When Joseph hit his lowest point, God poured out His relentless, unfailing love. I wish I knew how Joseph felt this love, but however he experienced it, God's care sustained him during those dark and lonely years.

When we experience demotions instead of promotions, when we work hard but have precious little to show for it, we, too, can lean on His unfailing love. Joseph had his dreams to give him hope, but we have something much more certain—God's inerrant Word. We have Jesus' presence in the Lord's Supper. Therefore, we can cling confidently to the truth of God's "everlasting love" (Jeremiah 31:3).

How God Measures Success

Some might interpret Joseph's story as a life lesson: work hard, and you will eventually achieve prominence and power. Hollywood movies love a rags-to-riches story. We all hope for greatness, so the story of the underdog rising up out of slavery, getting out of prison, and making something out of his life inspires us.

But that's not the point of Joseph's life. The main point of Joseph's story tells of the providence of God. Joseph's life had many confusing melodies and rhythms, but God orchestrated them into a composition singing of *His* glory. Potiphar, the jailer, and Pharaoh all recognized the Lord's presence with Joseph. In a land of superstition and false gods, Joseph's life sang the song of Yahweh, the one true God.

Joseph recognized this theme in his life. When his brothers feared Joseph would seek revenge for their mistreatment of him, he said, "Do not fear, for am I in the place of God? As for you, you meant evil against me, but God meant it for good, to bring it about that many people should be kept alive, as they are today" (Genesis 50:19–20).

TRUST THE LORD TO HELP YOU COMPLETE THE WORK HE HAS GIVEN YOU RIGHT NOW—WHETHER YOU DEEM THE JOB GREAT OR SMALL—AND YOU WILL HAVE SUCCESS IN HIS EYES.

Joseph's life demonstrates the providence of God, but it also illustrates how God measures success. Yes, God placed Joseph in a place of worldly influence, but when did God declare Joseph a success? When he lived life as a slave and a prisoner, a life not for himself but for others.

You don't need worldwide fame, bulging bank accounts, or impressive titles for God to declare your life a success. Trust the Lord to help you complete the work He has given you right now—whether you deem the job great or small—and you will have success in His eyes.

CHAPTER 2

RAHAB: RISQUÉ ROMANCER

TIMELINE

Joseph	1915 BC
Rahab	1406 BC

I heard the shofar blow. Again. I ran to the window and saw a procession outside the city wall. The sight of these foreigners marching around Jericho filled my heart with anxiety and with—how to say it?—a holy fear.

I had first experienced this feeling when I entertained two particular visitors in my inn. When drink had loosened their tongues, these men told stories of a great crowd on the other side of the Jordan River.

Map © iStock / Peter Hermes Furian

"There must be millions of people," they said with eyes wide. "And the tales we've heard! It is said that when they left Egypt forty years ago to escape Pharaoh, their God held back the waters of the Red Sea so they could cross on dry land ahead of Pharaoh's army! And more recently, the God of these Israelites defeated two powerful Amorite kings, Sihon and Og."

My heart had quickened at the talk of this God. I thought I understood gods: Carved figures people kept in their homes. Objects worshiped at festivals. Mysterious beings my neighbors believed controlled the harvest and weather.

But this God! A God who could command the sea and could defeat mighty kings. This God deserved attention.

The news about the Israelites spread through Jericho. Everyone was talking about them. The hearts of the people burned with fear—but not mine. My heart burned with a longing to know this God who worked wonders.

But would He want to know me? If this God only accepted important people, morally upstanding people, I would have no chance. Sure, men noticed me—but only for what they could get out of me. Everyone else turned away as I approached. My risqué reputation might cause the Israelites' God to also turn away.

I thought about what had happened only a few days before. My house was part of the city wall, so I could see what took place just outside the city. One night, I saw some visitors approach Jericho, so I stood outside my door to welcome them to my inn.

"Need a place to stay?" I asked as they passed by.

Yes, they did. They came in and ate my food—but refused my other services. Instead, they peppered me with questions about Jericho.

Then I heard a commotion outside in the street. Soldiers yelling, "Where are the spies? Have you seen the spies?"

It didn't take a genius to conclude that the men at my table were the very spies the soldiers were hunting. "Quick," I said. "Follow me." We ran up the stone stairs to the roof of my house. "Hide under these." I pointed to piles of flax drying. The men scrambled under the stalks, and I flew back down the stairs just as the king's men stormed through the door. "Bring out the men who just came to your house. They are spies."

In my business, I have a bit of practice in fabricating stories to protect my customers, and this experience helped me now. "It is true some foreigners came to me, but I didn't know where they were from. Just before the gate closed for the night, they decided to leave. If you hurry, you'll catch them."

After the soldiers left, I rushed back up to the roof and spoke to the men. "I know that Yahweh has given you this land. Fear has fallen on everyone here for we have heard all that your God has done. Surely, He is God in the heavens above and the earth beneath. Please, promise me that since I have helped you, you will be kind to me and my family. Please save us from death when you return."

The men promised they would protect me and my family if I told no one of their plans. They handed me a scarlet cord and told me to tie it in my window and to make sure my whole family was in the house. We hung the cord out my window, and then they climbed down and disappeared into the hills.

As the days passed, I wondered when they would return. Then today a group of people arrived outside Jericho. Some were dressed as soldiers, some in religious garb. Some carried a box on poles—a box adorned with angels. They said nothing and they stayed outside the city wall. But their ram's horns pierced the air.

Something was about to happen.

KEY VERSE

And as soon as we heard it, our hearts melted, and there was no spirit left in any man because of you, for the LORD your God, He is God in the heavens above and on the earth beneath. (Joshua 2:11)

In our everyday lives, we might be tempted to measure our success by the number of friends and social connections we have. As kids, perhaps we hoped the cool kids would notice us. In high school, we wanted prom dates and invitations to exclusive parties. Perhaps college meant joining a highly regarded sorority. And now, how good we feel about ourselves might fluctuate with the number of likes we get on social media.

Relationships are important, but God doesn't measure our personal success by how many friends we have. In this chapter, we'll examine the life of a woman who probably had many connections but not an abundance of real relationships. Yet, even though she might have been shunned socially, God chose her and used her faith in Him to bring success to His people.

SETTING THE SCENE

In the last chapter, we learned about Joseph and his brothers. The arrival of Joseph's family in Egypt began a four-hundred-year stay in that country. The descendants of Jacob multiplied, and after a time, Egypt's new pharaoh, who had forgotten about Joseph's role in saving the nation, enslaved the Israelites. After centuries of forced servitude, God raised up Moses to free His people and bring them back to the Promised Land.

When the people reached the border of that land, Moses sent spies into Canaan to observe and report back. The spies returned to the Israelite camp, full of fear of the giant people and walled cities they saw there. Their fear spread, and because the people lacked trust, the Lord sentenced them to forty years of wandering in the wilderness. Moses died in the wilderness, and his protégé, Joshua, took over the leadership.

Around 1406 BC, the people again arrived at the border of the Promised Land—right across the Jordan River from Jericho. This strategic city guarded the Jordan Valley and all the main routes into Canaan. It also controlled the region's only freshwater spring. Defeating Jericho would be the first step in taking over Canaan.

Sneaky Success

Like Moses before him, Joshua sent out two spies to observe the land. Once in Jericho, they came to Rahab's house. Rahab was, as they say, a lady of the evening. But before you think the worst of those two Israelite men, you should know that in those days prostitutes often served as innkeepers. Their homes were places to get food and to sleep (and maybe obtain some extra benefits). Plus, Rahab's house was part of the city wall. If the Israelite spies needed to make a quick escape, Rahab's house was the ideal location.

In antiquity, prostitutes often became involved in intelligence activities.[11] (In fact, Rahab may have been a spy too.) Since many outsiders passed through their establishments, they had access to a lot of information. Perhaps Rahab had cooperated in this exchange of news before, so when the king's men arrived at her door looking for the Israelite spies, they expected the spies to be there and her to hand them over. And maybe because of past assistance, they didn't doubt her when she said, "True, the men came to me, but I did not know where they were from. And when the gate was about to be closed at dark, the men went out. I do not know where the men went. Pursue them quickly, for you will overtake them" (Joshua 2:4–5).

As we read, Rahab had hidden the men under some flax stalks she had drying on her roof. Why would she protect these foreign spies instead of her own city? Why would she risk her life to save theirs?

Because she understood they represented a powerful God.

Her position as innkeeper had likely made her privy to conversations her guests had about a great throng of people on the other side of the Jordan River. Everything she heard convinced her that these two Israelite men were on the winning side, and she pleaded with them to save her and her family.

> WHY WOULD RAHAB PROTECT FOREIGN SPIES INSTEAD OF HER OWN CITY? BECAUSE SHE UNDERSTOOD THEY REPRESENTED A POWERFUL GOD.

The spies left, and Rahab saw no sign of the Israelites for days. Then one day she probably heard the sound of marching feet outside the city wall and a long blast on a ram's horn. Certainly the residents of Jericho shook at the eerie signal of the horn. But Rahab's declaration of God's power, "The LORD your God, He is God in the heavens above and on the earth beneath" (Joshua 2:11), makes me think that any fears she felt would have been subdued by the certainty that she would soon see something amazing.

THE WALLS OF JERICHO

On a trip to Israel, my husband and I visited Jericho. We learned it is the oldest inhabited city on earth, and we saw a round stone structure that archaeologists think dates to before Abraham!

White stone walls still stand at the site of Jericho. These walls supported the red brick walls that fell on the seventh day of the Israelites' marching. The walls fell outward, forming a ramp for the Israelites to enter the city.[12] Excavations at the site show evidence of an earthquake at the time of the collapse of the wall.[13] It is possible God used an earthquake to bring down the wall.

The Bible tells us that Rahab's house was a part of Jericho's wall. Most likely, the city wall was a casement wall consisting of two parallel walls. Rooms for living and storage could have been constructed between the parallel walls.[14]

But if the city wall fell, how did Rahab's house survive? Amazingly, excavations in 1907–1909 revealed a section of the wall that hadn't fallen. This portion stood as tall as eight feet high and still had houses built against it.[15] God made the rest of the wall fall flat and destroyed the entire city, but He saved one woman with tenacious faith, along with her family.

Seven days later, she did. The first six days, the Israelites marched around the city wall one time. The seventh day, however, they kept going. One, two, three . . . seven times. After the seventh lap, the Israelites shouted. The ground shook, bricks fell, and the city wall collapsed, but Rahab's house remained standing. The Israelites went back to the house and "brought out Rahab and her father and mother and brothers and all who belonged to her" (Joshua 6:23). Rahab and her family escaped destruction.

UNQUALIFIED FOR SUCCESS

Rahab's story intersects with the dramatic story of the fall of Jericho. When the Lord gave the land of Canaan to His chosen people, He commanded them to destroy the people living there because of their idolatry and extreme sins, which included child sacrifice and ritual prostitution. So if God planned to destroy the wicked, why did He save a prostitute?

God's grace shines as He chooses a broken, imperfect woman to further His plan for His chosen people and the world. Rahab was a sinner, no doubt about it. She led a life that was immoral. Improper. Indecent. Most likely, the majority of the citizens of Jericho shunned her. Yet God reached out—and gave her faith.

No other explanation for her declaration of trust exists. At the news of the Israelite throng, everyone else in Jericho shook in fear. Rahab told the spies, "Our hearts melted, and there was no spirit left in any man" (Joshua 2:11a). Yet, while the news about the Israelite God caused the courage of Rahab's neighbors to melt like butter, the same news led her to faith. She declared, "For the LORD your God, He is God in the heavens above and on the earth beneath" (v. 11b). The Lord gave her faith in spite of an atmosphere of fear.

Rahab became a key component in the success of the destruction of Jericho. Don't you love how God used a flawed woman? Her role in the defeat of Jericho demonstrates that God doesn't wait until we're accomplished, cleaned up, and respectable before He works through us. He uses us in our less-than-perfect state. Even when the world looks down on us,

GOD DOESN'T WAIT UNTIL WE'RE ACCOMPLISHED, CLEANED UP, AND RESPECTABLE BEFORE HE WORKS THROUGH US. shuns us, or overlooks us, He allows us to be a part of His plan to bring victory to His people and glory to His name.

I know a remarkable woman who can personally attest to God's grace. I met her when I volunteered at a transitional home where she and thirty other women were trying to rebuild their lives. She had spent forty years on the streets living a Rahab-style life filled with drugs and danger. But one day she met Jesus, and everything changed. The almighty God of heaven got hold of her heart, and drugs lost their grip on her soul.

After rehab, she came to the transitional home to learn basic life skills like writing a résumé and applying for a job. I tutored her for her GED, and I ended up learning a lot in the process. There, in a basement filled with mismatched chairs and sofas, she taught me about talking to and about God. This woman could pray! Quoting Scripture, she boldly called out to our powerful Father. This woman had passion! Her wonder and excitement for the Lord rubbed off on me, and she taught me about evangelism. If the two of us went out to run errands or have lunch, she never shied from telling the clerk, "Jesus loves you!"

As this woman grew in faith, she began to receive invitations to share her story. Her transformed life gave a vivid picture of God's grace and power. Although society would have measured her a dismal failure, the Lord used her to successfully bring His Good News to others.[16]

Immediate and Lasting Success

Rahab's faith brought immediate success. Her quick thinking saved the Israelite spies and led to an astounding triumph for the Israelite nation.

Her savvy also brought rescue for her family. They alone were saved. Joshua told the people, "The city and all that is within it shall be devoted to the Lord for destruction. Only Rahab the prostitute and all who are with her in her house shall live, because she hid the messengers whom we sent"

SEVEN DAYS OF MARCHING

God gave Joshua specific instructions for the destruction of Jericho:

> You shall march around the city, all the men of war going around the city once. Thus shall you do for six days. Seven priests shall bear seven trumpets of rams' horns before the ark. On the seventh day you shall march around the city seven times, and the priests shall blow the trumpets. And when they make a long blast with the ram's horn, when you hear the sound of the trumpet, then all the people shall shout with a great shout, and the wall of the city will fall down flat, and the people shall go up, everyone straight before him. (Joshua 6:3–5)

I can imagine the Israelites asking, "Why all this marching?"

One reason for the seven days and the seven laps on the last day could be the biblical significance of the number seven, which often signifies completion or perfection. God created the world in six days and rested on the seventh. Jesus spoke seven statements from the cross. God gave messages to seven churches in Revelation. Here in Joshua, God also told Joshua to have seven priests and seven trumpets.

But consider that God may have instructed the Israelites to march for seven days to test their obedience. Maybe the first day when the Israelites marched around Jericho, its residents trembled in fear at the sound of the rams' horns. But perhaps on the following days the people inside the wall lost some of their fear and jeered at the people outside the wall when all they did was march. The Israelites could have grown impatient with the daily parade and picked up swords instead of shofars.

God also used the seven days of marching "to impress deeply upon the people the fact that it was the almighty power and faithfulness of Jehovah alone which gave into their hands this fortified city."[17] The marching made no earthly sense. But it

helped the children of Israel learn that victory did not depend
on their might—only on God's.

(Joshua 6:17). Because Jericho was the first city the Israelites conquered, everything inside it was dedicated to the Lord.[18] At first, Rahab and her family probably stayed outside the camp of Israel because anything unclean would not have been allowed to enter (Leviticus 13:46). According to the instructions described in Numbers 31:19 for captives of war, they likely remained outside the camp for seven days and completed purification rights on the third and seventh days. After that, Rahab lived in Israel, spared because "she hid the messengers whom Joshua sent to spy out Jericho" (Joshua 6:25).

Rahab's actions not only brought immediate success; her faith in God brought success she probably didn't know about in her lifetime. In his Gospel, Matthew mentions Rahab again: "And Salmon the father of Boaz by Rahab, and Boaz the father of Obed by Ruth, and Obed the father of Jesse, and Jesse the father of David the king" (Matthew 1:5–6). That's right; not only did Rahab live among God's chosen people, but she was the great-great-grandmother of King David.

That Matthew passage is part of the genealogy of Jesus. God chose Rahab, a messed-up, imperfect, unqualified person, to carry the DNA of His beloved Son when Jesus took on human form. Amazing.

Once again, God shows His grace in using flawed people to influence the world.

WHEN YOU FEEL FLAWED

Your past probably isn't like Rahab's. Yet we all have past sins that haunt us, imperfections that leave us feeling inept and falling short. Perhaps your feelings of brokenness stem from a characteristic or trait you wish you could change. Or maybe you grew up hearing you would never make anything of yourself so often that you started to believe it.

A SCARLET CORD

When the spies escaped from the king's men through Rahab's window, they told her, "Behold, when we come into the land, you shall tie this scarlet cord in the window through which you let us down" (Joshua 2:18). The cord served the practical purpose of identifying Rahab's house. But look more closely and you'll see additional significance. In the time between the spies' flight from Jericho and their return, the Israelites celebrated the Passover (Joshua 5:10). Part of this important festival commemorating the escape from Egypt involved sacrificing a perfect lamb and painting the doorposts and lintels of their houses with the lamb's blood (see Exodus 12:3–7). The streaks of scarlet blood helped them remember that at the first Passover, the blood of the lamb was the sign for the Lord to pass over that house and spare the firstborn.

The blood also represented the salvation that would come through the Savior. Peter writes, "You were ransomed from the futile ways inherited from your forefathers, not with perishable things such as silver or gold, but with the precious blood of Christ, like that of a lamb without blemish or spot" (1 Peter 1:18–19). The scarlet thread that hung from Rahab's window and saved her and her family can picture Christ's scarlet blood that saved you and me.[19]

Another beautiful truth becomes apparent when we look at the words for "scarlet thread" in the original language. The Hebrew reads šānî ḥûṭ tiqvâ, translated literally as "scarlet thread line." Interestingly, while tiqvâ is translated here as "thread" or "line," it can also mean "hope" or "expectation" (from blueletterbible.com). Psalm 71:5 reads, "For You, O Lord, are my hope [tiqvâ], my trust, O LORD, from my youth." The scarlet blood of Christ gives us hope and fills us with expectation for the joy of heaven.

That's why Rahab's story gives us hope. God used her flawed life to work out success for her, her family, and millions of Israelites. He chose this unqualified woman to bring triumph to future generations through her great-great-grandson David and eternal victory to the world through the Son of God.

So what can we learn from Rahab's life when we start to believe our flaws disqualify us from success in God's kingdom?

Remember that God uses imperfect people. If I were in God's position, I doubt I would have chosen a prostitute to save my people. I'll bet a city councilman or prominent merchant also had a home in the city wall and could have used his influence to save the spies. God could have chosen to work through an "important" person.

GOD CAN TAKE YOUR SHAME AND INADEQUACIES AND TURN THEM INTO SPECTACULAR TRIUMPH.

But He chose Rahab. The Bible emphasizes that God uses broken people when it mentions Rahab in the New Testament. Hebrews 11:31 and James 2:25 both praise this Old Testament woman even as they identify her as "Rahab the prostitute." You'd think after six hundred years and becoming an ancestor of both King David and the King of kings, the poor woman could get a break from her shameful past. But it reminds us that we are not judged by our flaws. We are measured by grace. God loves broken people. He can take the shame and inadequacies of His baptized and forgiven daughters and turn them into spectacular triumph.

Realize it's *faith* in an almighty God that brings success. Those New Testament references that speak of Rahab as a prostitute also praise her faith. Hebrews 11:31 says:

> By faith Rahab the prostitute did not perish with those who were disobedient, because she had given a friendly welcome to the spies.

Without faith in Yahweh, Rahab would not have risked her life to save the lives of the spies.

James, who emphasizes that "faith by itself, if it does not have works, is dead" (James 2:17), speaks of Rahab's faith in action:

> And in the same way was not also Rahab the prostitute justified by works when she received the messengers and sent them out by another way? (James 2:25)

We also witness Rahab's faith in her own words. In the longest prose speech by any woman in the Bible, Rahab told the spies:

> "I know that the LORD has given you the land, and that the fear of you has fallen upon us, and that all the inhabitants of the land melt away before you. For we have heard how the LORD dried up the water of the Red Sea before you when you came out of Egypt, and what you did to the two kings of the Amorites who were beyond the Jordan, to Sihon and Og, whom you devoted to destruction. And as soon as we heard it, our hearts melted, and there was no spirit left in any man because of you, for the LORD your God, He is God in the heavens above and on the earth beneath. Now then, please swear to me by the LORD that, as I have dealt kindly with you, you also will deal kindly with my father's house, and give me a sure sign that you will save alive my father and mother, my brothers and sisters, and all who belong to them, and deliver our lives from death." And the men said to her, "Our life for yours even to death! If you do not tell this business of ours, then when the LORD gives us the land we will deal kindly and faithfully with you." (Joshua 2:9–14)

Rahab repeatedly uses the covenant name of God indicated in our modern Bibles by the name *LORD* (in capital letters). This stands for *Yahweh*, the name God told Moses at the burning bush. Rahab didn't have faith in a generic god. She trusted in the one true God. Hearing of Yahweh's mighty actions against the powerful rulers of the day convinced her He would give her land to the people of Israel. She proclaims, "The LORD your God, He is God in the heavens above and on the earth beneath" (Joshua 2:11).

Faith in an almighty God turns our lives around. The world tells us to believe in *ourselves*, but what brings true success is an unwavering trust in the Lord of heaven and earth. Faith in the One who can defeat worldly powers and our own challenges. Confidence in the Lord who can flatten cities and obliterate our problems that seem like impenetrable walls.

When we trust in God's power, we can do whatever task He has given us—even the equivalent of knocking down a fortress. The apostle Paul wrote, "And God is able to make all grace abound to you, so that having all sufficiency in all things at all times, you may abound in every good work" (2 Corinthians 9:8).

THE WORLD TELLS US TO BELIEVE IN *OURSELVES*. BUT WHAT BRINGS TRUE SUCCESS IS AN UNWAVERING TRUST IN THE LORD OF HEAVEN AND EARTH.

Know that you may not see the success your faith brings about. Rahab saw an immediate result of her faith in the saving of the Israelite spies and her own family. But I doubt she lived to see her great-great-grandson become king of Israel, and she would have had no clue that she would become an ancestor of the Savior of the world. We can't always witness the results of a faithful life.

Perhaps you think, *I'm only a stay-at-home mom to a couple of unruly boys.* But consider a possible scenario. One of those boys grows up to become a teacher. His kindness leads one of the boys in his class to believe in Christ. As a teenager, this young man volunteers at a soup kitchen, where he befriends a drug addict who learns about the grace of God and turns her life around. Years later, this former drug addict teaches a Bible study at her church, where her remarkable story inspires a young woman who was visiting the church. This young woman joins the congregation and takes her children to church every Sunday so they can learn about the life-changing Gospel. One of her sons . . .

We can't know the full extent of God's works through our frailties and flaws. We can only trust that He will work through us as we act with His gift of faith in our hearts.

THE VICTORY IS ALREADY YOURS

The first words Rahab speaks to the Israelites spies are "I know that the LORD has given you the land" (Joshua 2:9). She is certain they will be victorious.

Joshua hears similar words from God Himself: "See, I have given Jericho into your hand" (Joshua 6:2). The tense of the Hebrew verb shows that the battle is already won. Can you imagine the confidence this gave Joshua?

We have that same assurance. What battles are you fighting? Wars against physical illness? Skirmishes against nagging doubt? Encounters with difficult people? Confrontations against paralyzing fear? Listen to Jesus' words to His disciples on the night before His crucifixion: "I have said these things to you, that in Me you may have peace. In the world you will have tribulation. But take heart; I have overcome the world" (John 16:33). Jesus wanted to give certainty of ultimate victory to these men who would face doubt and fear in the coming days plus suffering and persecution in the coming years. His words also give us confidence. Yes, the bad news is that here on earth, we will have sickness, problems, and conflicts. But oh, the Good News! Jesus has already fought the battle for us and won. He has guaranteed victory over every heartache and anxiety. Live like the victory is already yours.

HOW GOD MEASURES SUCCESS

Before the fall of Jericho, no one would have described Rahab's life as a success. As a prostitute, she most likely lived as a social outcast. No one would have chosen her for a position of honor. If she had applied for

SUCCESS IN GOD'S KINGDOM DOES NOT DEPEND ON OUR QUALIFICATIONS. the job of ancestor to the Savior of the world, her shortcomings would have outnumbered her qualifications.

But God made Rahab's life prosper. He gave her grace, gave her faith, gave her a place among His chosen people, and gave her a place in the family line of kings—including the King of kings.

The Lord doesn't measure success by our social connections. Whatever position in life you have right now—honored or humble, influential or inconsequential—God sees you as an important piece of His plan to make His glory known. He will use you to demonstrate His grace.

Success in God's kingdom does not depend on our qualifications.

CHAPTER 3

DAVID: SUPERSIZE SINNER

TIMELINE

Joseph	1915 BC
Rahab	1406 BC
David	1010 BC

A cry of pain in the next room sent David to his knees. How he wanted to go in to see Bathsheba! But the midwife had sent him out of the room. "This is women's work," she said.

All David could do was wait. And pray.

He got up from his knees. As Bathsheba labored to give birth to their child, he paced and thought of God's many blessings to him. The victories over lions and bears as he watched the family sheep. Triumph over Goliath who dared to defy the

Map © iStock / Peter Hermes Furian

living God. Conquest over the Philistines time and time again. A sumptuous palace, beautiful family, and kingship of God's people. Without Yahweh, David knew none of these successes would be his.

Would God bless him one more time? Would the Lord show compassion and allow this new baby to survive? David knew he did not deserve it. After all God had given him, David had almost thrown it all away.

David had first seen Bathsheba from his rooftop. Her beauty had immediately captivated him. She was bathing, so he should have turned away. He should have been satisfied with the wives already in his palace. But he had to have *her*. A red flag had waved when someone said, "Isn't she the *wife* of Uriah the Hittite?" Why had he chosen to ignore that little word? Oh, the pain he had caused!

He thought one passionate night with the beautiful woman would be the end. But a few weeks later, Bathsheba informed David of her pregnancy. Now what?

He had strayed so far from God's ways that he fooled himself into believing he could cover up his sin. But, of course, that only got him into deeper trouble. How could he have considered it a good idea to send Bathsheba's husband to a certain death in battle just to save his own reputation?

Lord, have mercy.

David remembered how God had graciously sent the prophet Nathan to confront his sin. And when David saw that not only had he crossed the line with Bathsheba and Uriah but he had also broken God's holy Commandments, he confessed to Nathan: "I have sinned against the Lord." He recalled the relief he felt when Nathan responded, "The Lord also has put away your sin. You won't die."

Yet he experienced consequences. The beautiful son born out of his sin with Bathsheba had died. And now, as he heard her shrieks of pain, he wondered, *Will this baby live? Will God have mercy on us?*

Then he heard a different wail—the cry of an infant! *Thank You, heavenly Father!*

2 sam 12:1-10

David resumed his pacing until Bathsheba's maid emerged from the room and invited him in. He approached Bathsheba's bed and gingerly sat on the edge to hold her and to peer at the little bundle in her arms.

"It's a boy," she whispered through tears that spoke happiness.

David bent his head toward hers and gazed at their son.

"What will you name him?" the midwife asked.

David smiled at Bathsheba and said, "Solomon. We pray that he is a man of peace."

The prophet Nathan knocked at the open door and peered in. "The Lord has sent me," he said. "Yahweh has given this child another name— Jedidiah, which means 'beloved of the Lord.'"

> ### KEY VERSE
> Then King David went in and sat before the LORD and said, "Who am I, O Lord GOD, and what is my house, that You have brought me thus far?" (2 Samuel 7:18)

Our culture often measures success by victory in the political arena. Candidates run for office and one election declares them a success or failure. Will the people trust them to govern, or will they deny them the power to lead?

David didn't set out to become a ruler; God put him in that powerful position. David experienced astounding success as king, but looking at his significant spiritual catastrophes, how did God measure his success?

SETTING THE SCENE

We can read David's story in 1 and 2 Samuel, 1 Kings, and 1 Chronicles. And we see his heart in the songs he wrote in the Book of Psalms. Scripture arguably tells us more about David than any other biblical character.[20]

I have heard scholars declare that one compelling reason to accept the Bible as true is that it doesn't gloss over the imperfections of the people of God. While sacred books of other religions might whitewash the morality of their leaders, the Bible displays its characters' flaws as a way to highlight God's grace.

We see this played out in the life of David. At times, the Bible presents him as the larger-than-life hero—slaying giants, defeating armies, winning at every turn. But the Bible also reveals his failures—the supersize sinner who disobeys God's laws and fails his family, all of which leads to horrific death and disorder. Yet God identifies him as "a man after His own heart" (1 Samuel 13:14).

David's very lineage speaks of God's grace. Born around 1040 BC, he was the great-great-grandson of Rahab, the heroine of our last chapter. God demonstrated His grace as He chose a former prostitute who married an Israelite and gave birth to Boaz, who married a Moabite refugee named Ruth, who gave birth to Obed, who became the father of Jesse, who was the father of David.

Although David had a grand life and a prominent place in history, he had humble beginnings. When God sent the prophet Samuel to the home of Jesse to anoint one of his eight sons as Israel's next king, Jesse didn't even call the youngest in from shepherding the flocks. But when the baby of the family entered the room, Samuel said, "He's the one."

When we look at David's life through his amazing successes like his battle with Goliath and victories over the Philistines, we agree that God made a fine decision when He chose this shepherd boy. But when we dig deeper, we find so many failures that we wonder how the Lord could see David as a man after His own heart.

GIANT SUCCESS

When my kids were little, they loved playing David and Goliath. I can still picture my pint-size four-year-old calling out in his gruffest voice, "Who are you that you come to fight with me?" This "scary" Goliath donned a bucket as a helmet, waved a cheerleading baton as a sword, and bellowed to his seven-year-old sister, who played the part of David. She swung a lime-green jump rope as a sling and shouted, "I come to you in the name of the living God!"

With our family room as the theater, my kids acted out the story of David and Goliath countless times. They knew the lines by heart from Sunday School lessons and animated Bible videos. They took turns playing the characters, but the favorite role by far was David, because who doesn't want to be the winner?

> WE WANT THE ROLE OF THE ONE WHO DEFEATS THE BIG GUYS IN OUR WAY AND RISES VICTORIOUS IN THE FACE OF ENORMOUS ODDS.

Perhaps that's why we love the story of David and Goliath. We feel small in a world of giant challenges and monumental obstacles. We want the role of the one who defeats the big guys in our way and rises victorious in the face of enormous odds.

I offer that role to you right now. Picture yourself as that shepherd boy. Your father has sent you to check on your three older brothers who have gone to fight the Philistines. When you arrive, you find your brothers camped with the rest of the troops on a hill on one side of the Valley of Elah. On the opposite side of the valley, the Philistine army lines up for battle. All of the enemy soldiers look terrifying, but one man turns every Israelite knee to lentil soup. A giant of a man—nine feet tall—with a bronze helmet, 125 pounds of body armor, and a 15-pound bronze javelin declares himself the champion of the Philistines and challenges someone from the Israelite army to fight him one-on-one. Your brothers inform you that this giant, Goliath, has done this routine for forty days. No one has accepted the challenge. In fact, as they tell you this, they and the rest of the Israelite army have turned and run.

Incredulous—not at the lack of courage but at the lack of faith—you ask, "Who is this uncircumcised Philistine, that he should defy the armies of the living God?" (1 Samuel 17:26). Your brothers tease you, saying you're merely a kid, but you march over to King Saul's tent and say, "I'll fight Goliath!" You remember how God has saved you from lions and bears while you guarded the sheep. Certainly God can also defeat this Goliath.

King Saul gives his blessing—and his armor. But the armor fits like a tin can on a mouse, and instead you grab your shepherd's staff and sling. At the nearby stream, you select five smooth stones as ammunition. Who needs a helmet or a coat of mail when God provides all the protection?

Time to face the music. You start walking across the broad valley and the Philistine giant begins his approach. He snickers and says, "Am I a dog that you come to me with sticks?" (v. 43). This only fuels your resolve to demonstrate the power of Yahweh. You shout back, "You come to me with a sword and with a spear and with a javelin, but I come to you in the name of the LORD of hosts, the God of the armies of Israel, whom you have defied" (v. 45). And before the giant realizes what is happening, you grab a stone from your bag and hurl it with your sling. The stone lands smack-dab in the middle of Goliath's forehead, and his nine-foot body crashes to the ground. Only one thing left to do. You cut off Goliath's head with his own sword.

DAVID OOZED CONFIDENCE BECAUSE HE KNEW HIS SECRET WEAPON.

Imagine David's elation at having defeated that giant. Imagine the joy in the triumph. Now imagine the reaction of the people watching. A young shepherd had succeeded where no one else dared. How was this possible?

First of all, David knew God. Although he had the lowliest job in the family (shepherds were at the very bottom of the corporate ladder), watching sheep gave David plenty of time to spend with God. He probably filled his long days in the fields by practicing his harp and composing songs of praise to Yahweh. He vividly experienced God's protection when the Lord helped him defeat wild animals attacking the sheep. David knew God as a God of love, strength, and security.

A LONG STRING OF SUCCESSES

David's victory over Goliath began a long string of wins for David.

- **Success as an army commander.** After David slayed Goliath, Saul made him a commander of a thousand men who defeated the Philistines again and again (1 Samuel 18:13–14).

- **Success at Keilah.** When King Saul saw David's success, he grew jealous and tried to kill David. While hiding from Saul in the wilderness, David heard of a Philistine raid on the city of Keilah. God enabled David to defeat the entire Philistine army with a few hundred men (1 Samuel 23:1–5).

- **Successful rescue.** When David and his men were away from their homes in Ziklag, Amalekites raided the city and took all the women and children. David and his ragtag bunch hunted down and defeated the marauding Amalekites, rescuing all of the captives (1 Samuel 30).

- **Successful coronation.** After King Saul died, God instructed David to go to Hebron, where the men of Judah anointed him as their king (2 Samuel 2:1–4).

- **Successful unification of the nation.** For seven and a half years, David reigned over Judah, while Saul's son Ish-bosheth ruled the other eleven tribes. After Ish-bosheth was murdered, all the tribes of Israel came to David and made him their king (2 Samuel 5:1–5).

- **Successful capture of Jerusalem.** David captured the almost impregnable stronghold of Jerusalem and made it the new capital of Israel (2 Samuel 5:6–10).

- **Successful military victories.** David experienced many triumphs as he defeated the Philistines, the Syrians, the Edomites, and the forces of Hadadezer (2 Samuel 5:17–25; 8:1–14).

> When we examine these triumphs, we notice a pattern. Over and over, Scripture says David "inquired of the LORD" (1 Samuel 23:2, 4; 30:8; 2 Samuel 2:1; 5:19, 23). He also recognized "that the LORD had established him king over Israel, and that He had exalted His kingdom for the sake of His people Israel" (2 Samuel 5:12). David didn't assume he could succeed on his own. Over and over, he asked the Lord for direction because he knew victory came only with God on his side.

Second, David did not fight Goliath in order to acquire fame or riches for himself. When he arrived at the Israelite camp, the soldiers told him, "The king will enrich the man who kills him with great riches and will give him his daughter and make his father's house free in Israel" (v. 25). But David hardly cared about that. He fought for God's honor. His reply? "Who is this uncircumcised Philistine, that he should defy the armies of the living God?" (v. 26).

Third, David didn't depend on man-made weapons or strategies. Saul offered the royal armor, but David declined and grabbed his staff and a few stones instead. Even though Goliath disdained him and practically laughed at the "stick" David brought to the fight, David oozed confidence because he knew his secret weapon: "You come to me with a sword and with a spear and with a javelin, but I come to you in the name of the LORD of hosts, the God of the armies of Israel, whom you have defied. This day the LORD will deliver you into my hand, and I will strike you down and cut off your head" (vv. 45–46).

When we face our own giants, let's use David's strategy. Spend so much time in God's Word that you know beyond a shadow of a doubt how much God cares for you. Learn about His unbeatable strength and His promised protection. Soak up His love and rest in His comfort. Then fight not for your own honor but to demonstrate God's grace in your life. Focus on bringing glory to the Lord instead of fame for yourself. Don't trust in the ill-fitting armor of self-help books or podcasts. Put your faith in the Lord who has already defeated your greatest enemies—sin, eternal damnation, and the wiles of the evil one—for you. We find success not in ourselves but in the Lord who continually fights for us.

SUPERSIZE FAILURES

Even though David had almost superhuman success, he also had supersize failures. Perhaps the biggest failure—and the one that led to so many other tragedies—was the one that began as a steamy love story. David saw Bathsheba and was smitten. When his one-night stand resulted in a surprise pregnancy, he arranged for her husband to be sent to the front lines where he was sure to be killed. Someone looking at the story of David and Goliath next to the story of David and Bathsheba might wonder, *Are these two Davids even the same person?*

David's horrendous sin resulted in other failures. Not long after he and Bathsheba wed and Bathsheba gave birth to Solomon, problems arose among David's older children. David had many wives and at least seventeen sons (2 Samuel 3:2–5 and 5:13–16). John R. Mittelstaedt, in his commentary on 1 and 2 Samuel, writes, "It is a tragic fact of David's life that his disregard for what God had to say about marriage brought him untold grief and heartache. David became a victim of his own sinful lifestyle."[21]

The tragic story begins in 2 Samuel 13:1: "Now Absalom, David's son, had a beautiful sister, whose name was Tamar. And after a time Amnon, David's son, loved her." Amnon's love turned into an insatiable lust that resulted in his violating his virgin half sister. King David, their father, was angry but did nothing. Meanwhile, Tamar's brother Absalom (who shared the same mother), seethed. "Absalom hated Amnon, because he had violated his sister Tamar" (v. 22).

Two years later, Absalom—still harboring hate for this half brother—decided to host a big party, inviting all of the king's sons and daughters. Because Amnon didn't know murder was on the menu, he showed up to the party. After Amnon was drunk on wine, Absalom ordered his servants to kill him.

Absalom realized the trouble he was in and fled to Geshur. After three years, David allowed Absalom to come home but refused to see him for another two years. Again, David did nothing—neither punishing Absalom for murdering Amnon nor accepting Absalom's actions as justice for Tamar and forgiving him.

In the meantime, Absalom began scheming to take over the throne. For four years, he positioned himself at the city gate and told anyone who entered, "Sorry, the king can't hear your case today. Oh, but if *I* were king, you would surely have justice!"

At the end of the four years, Absalom declared himself king of Israel. David fled Jerusalem with his family and servants. Eventually, he mustered troops to fight against Absalom's men. The Bible records the sad ending to the story. Although David defeated Absalom's men, "the loss there was great on that day, twenty thousand men" (2 Samuel 18:7). The casualties included Absalom, who got caught in the branches of a great oak. As he hung suspended in the air, David's general, Joab, killed him.

What do all of these failures have in common? When we looked at David's success, we noticed a pattern: David knew God, sought the honor of God, and depended on God's wisdom and strength. But when we look at the catastrophes and transgressions in his life, we see the opposite.

First, David appears to have forgotten God. When David sinned with Bathsheba, it seems he avoided God for a time. Although he tried to cover up his sin, on some level he realized the seriousness of his actions. "This time of silence and duplicity turned out to be a low point in David's spiritual life. He who had poured out his heart to God in prayer now allowed his prayer life to become virtually nonexistent. It doesn't appear as though David wrote a single psalm during this period."[22]

Second, where David previously fought for the honor of God, he now seems to bask in his own glory. At his first battle, he told Goliath, "This day the LORD will deliver you into my hand, and I will strike you down and cut off your head. And I will give the dead bodies of the host of the Philistines this day to the birds of the air and to the wild beasts of the earth, that all the earth may know that there is a God in Israel" (1 Samuel 17:46). But after he experienced victory after victory, the king of Israel didn't even go with the army to fight the Ammonites. Perhaps he began to believe his own public relations. When he heard the people sing, "Saul has struck down his thousands, and David his ten thousands" (1 Samuel 18:7), he may have started to believe there was nothing he couldn't do. And nothing he couldn't have. David's affair with Bathsheba came at the height of his success. No longer the humble shepherd boy, he had grown accustomed to getting everything he wanted.

Third, it appears he depended on his own wisdom and strength, rather than the Lord's. After the affair with Bathsheba, we find no sign that David "inquired of the LORD." In his earlier days, he often asked Yahweh, "What should I do next? Should I fight this battle? Where should I go?" But when his family sank into deep trouble, the Bible doesn't record David seeking the wisdom of God. The events that followed split his family *and* resulted in twenty thousand Israelites dying in a bloody battle.

CONFRONTING OUR OWN FAILURES

Our own failures may pale in comparison with David's, but we've all messed up. We've all ignored the Law written on our hearts and done the rotten deed anyway.

WHEN HIS FAMILY SANK INTO DEEP TROUBLE, THE BIBLE DOESN'T RECORD DAVID ASKING GOD ABOUT THE NEXT STEP.

My own list of failures could fill a hard drive, but perhaps my biggest regret comes from a time in high school. Just as David's worst mistake happened at the height of his success, my major mess-up occurred when I had experienced an important achievement.

My bookish nature means I love to learn. Give me a topic to study, and I'll hit the books until I understand the material. By the end of high school, my study habits had landed me at the top of my class. And like David, I started to act entitled. I *expected* to get the coveted spot of addressing my

THE DRIVE FOR SUCCESS AND THE PUSH TO GET WHAT WE WANT CAN SHUT OUR EARS TO THE HOLY SPIRIT'S RE-PROVING VOICE.

class at the graduation ceremony, and I was completely blindsided when someone else received that honor. The rejection hurt. That one of my best friends was chosen over me magnified the pain. I'm ashamed to say that not only did I complain to school officials about the perceived slight, but I gave my friend the silent treatment.

Why dredge up this old story? Because it demonstrates how the push to get what we want can shut our ears to reason and to the Holy Spirit's reproving voice. I knew I was failing big-time with the Lord's command to love my neighbor as myself. I knew that, as a Christian, I should rejoice with those who rejoice and not hold a grudge. But I let my need for recognition turn me into a spiteful, jealous person.

When has your drive for success shut out the gentle voice of the Spirit? When has desire for an earthly prize led you to ignore God's whisper in your soul?

When You Feel like a Failure

We've all been there. We've all taken a wrong turn in life. How does God respond when His GPS points the way we should go and we mute the direction, then plow into disaster? David's story gives us hope for when we fail. It offers these words of instruction:

Remember that God offers forgiveness. After the Bathsheba-and-Uriah disaster, God could have abandoned David. Instead, the Lord sent His prophet Nathan with a message. Rather than confronting the king with a fire-and-brimstone sermon, Nathan told a heart-stirring story about a rich man who stole an impoverished neighbor's lamb for his own feast. When David's anger flared against the injustice, Nathan said, "You are the man!" (2 Samuel 12:7). David repented and admitted, "I have sinned against the LORD" (v. 13a). Then Nathan delivered the good news: "The LORD also has put away your sin; you shall not die" (v. 13b).

Our heavenly Father offers us the same forgiveness when we repent. Looking back at my high school story, I needed to acknowledge that I not only hurt my friend but also ignored God's command to love as He loves. Eventually, the Holy Spirit bored through my wall of bitterness. When I finally owned up to my sin, I asked my friend for forgiveness, which she kindly gave. I repented to God and rejoiced that Jesus' death and resurrection allow me to be measured by His grace and not by my sins.

Rejoice that God doesn't withdraw His love when we fail. After David repented, God forgave him. But he and Bathsheba still had to pay the price for their sin. Nathan announced the punishment: "Because by this deed you have utterly scorned the LORD, the child who is born to you shall die" (v. 14). However, God demonstrated His continued love for David when Bathsheba gave birth to another son. The parents named the new baby Solomon. But the Bible tells us of another name: "And the LORD loved him and sent a message by Nathan the prophet. So he called his name Jedidiah, because of the LORD" (vv. 24–25). I absolutely love this part of the story. God showed His grace to David by giving the baby a name that means "beloved of the Lord"! And to further show His love and forgiveness, God made *this* son heir to the throne and part of the lineage of His own beloved Son.

God doesn't hand out His love and then say, "Never mind. I take that back." The Bible tells us He "shows His love for us in that while we were still sinners, Christ died for us" (Romans 5:8). The Lord loves mess-ups and sinners. Our failures do not disqualify us from God's love.

> THE LORD LOVES MESS-UPS AND SINNERS. OUR FAILURES DO NOT DISQUALIFY US FROM GOD'S LOVE.

Rest in the truth that you don't need to do something great for God. After David had become king over all of Israel, beaten back the Philistines, and settled in his own palace, he decided to do something great for God. He decided he needed to build God a new house.

King David ran his idea past Nathan, and the prophet gave him the go-ahead. But later that night God revealed a different message. The next day Nathan told David that God didn't want David to make a new house for Him. Instead, God declared, "I will make for you a great name, like the name of the great ones of the earth" (2 Samuel 7:9). God nixed David's plan. "The Lord tells David and Nathan not what they will do but what He will do and make for David—an everlasting house and kingdom."[23]

When we have done something wrong, we might think we can make up for it by doing something good for God. This might come from a motivation to show appreciation for His forgiveness, or it might come from self-serving interests to show God and others how contrite we are.

Eugene Peterson writes:

> There are times when our grand human plans to do something for God are seen, after a night of prayer, to be a huge human distraction from what God is doing for us.[24]

God told David, "You don't need to do something great for Me. Instead, sit back and watch. Your life is successful when it demonstrates what *I* can do—not what you can do."

God's Measure of Success

David as king would rate a high score on the world's success meter. But how did he measure up in God's eyes?

Scripture says that David was a man after God's own heart. That phrase comes from Samuel's words to King Saul after Saul sinned by offering a sacrifice that only Levites were allowed to perform: "Your kingdom shall not continue. The Lord has sought out a man after His own heart, and the Lord has commanded him to be prince over His people, because you have not kept what the Lord commanded you" (1 Samuel 13:14). We wonder how God could reject Saul for such a seemingly insignificant failing and then accept David with his supersize sins. After so many failures, how could the Lord see David as a man after His own heart?

In his commentary, Mittelstaedt makes the case that David could continue as someone God could use because of his sensitivity to God's Spirit.[25] Unlike Saul, who only made excuses when told of his sin, David repented. When confronted with his iniquities and failures, David admitted his guilt and sought God's forgiveness. After his sin with Bathsheba, David composed a beautiful song of contrition:

> Have mercy on me, O God,
>   according to Your steadfast love;
> according to Your abundant mercy
>   blot out my transgressions.
> Wash me thoroughly from my iniquity,
>   and cleanse me from my sin! (Psalm 51:1–2)

In the waters of Baptism, we also receive cleansing from our sin. God will not disqualify me from His family when I ignore His instructions. Instead, He will gently show me my sin, lead me to repent, then mercifully take me back in His arms.

The name *David* means "beloved."[26] And perhaps Scripture characterizes David as the type of man God was looking for because he lived out of that position of being loved by the Lord and responded by loving God in return.

David wrote seventy-three psalms, and fifty-three times in his psalms, David uses the word *hesed,* the Hebrew word translated as "steadfast love, unfailing love, or loving kindness." David's confidence in God's unending love shines in Psalm 86:15:

> But You, O Lord, are a God merciful and gracious,
> slow to anger and abounding in steadfast love and faithfulness.

Although David knew he had failed miserably and committed terrible sins, he also knew that he could come back to God because of the Lord's mercy, grace, faithfulness, and love. Despite his many faults and shortcomings, David's life demonstrated a life measured by grace.[27]

TO BE COUNTED AS A WOMAN AFTER GOD'S OWN HEART, I DON'T NEED TO BE PERFECT—JUST FORGIVEN!

Have you failed big-time? Have you ignored the Holy Spirit's voice in your heart and done something you now deeply regret? Do your shortcomings make you fear God's rejection?

David's story reassures us. Although this shepherd boy–turned–king failed again and again, God continued to love him, continued to use him to further His kingdom. Our supersize sins and failures do not necessarily derail us from God's plan. If we repent and receive the Lord's forgiveness, His grace can erase our guilt and redeem what's left of our lives.

Because of Jesus, God also gives us the name Beloved. When we mess up, may we recall God's unfailing love for us demonstrated in the gift of His Son. May we turn up the volume on the voice of the Holy Spirit by spending more time in God's Word and receiving the renewal offered in the Lord's Supper. May we repent and return to the Lord and let our lives reveal the grace of God.

To be counted as a woman after God's own heart, I don't need to be perfect—just forgiven!

CHAPTER 4

JEREMIAH:
POORLY RECEIVED PROPHET

TIMELINE

Joseph	1915 BC
Rahab	1406 BC
David	1010 BC
Jeremiah	628 BC

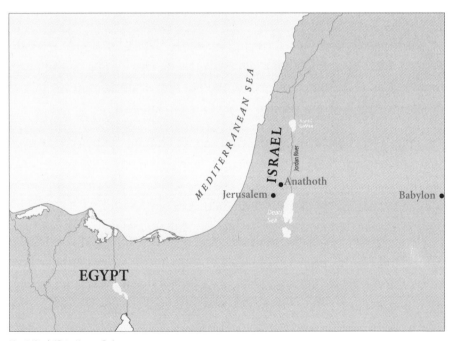

Map © iStock / Peter Hermes Furian

Mud, mud, and more mud.

Jeremiah's feet sank into deep muck. He couldn't pull his feet from the sludge, much less drag himself out of the cistern. Although this cistern was designed to catch rainwater, it now held only mud—and him, a persecuted prophet.

Jeremiah reflected on the irony: *I'm going to die in a place that once held life-giving water.*

Jeremiah knew his latest prophecies had angered some people enough that they wanted to make sure he never got out of this place. As the mud rose above his ankles, he thought back on what had brought him to this sinking situation.

Decades before, God had appointed him to the role of prophet. And Jeremiah had objected, "Lord, I'm too young! Plus, I get tongue-tied!" But God had reassured him: "Don't let your fear get in the way. I will walk with you wherever I send you."

At the time, Jeremiah thought the words "Don't be afraid" were directed only at his trepidation at speaking. He had no idea he had so much more to fear. Over the years, people had put him in stocks, thrown him in dungeons, kept him imprisoned, and plotted to kill him.

Plus, it had been a lonely life. God had told him not to marry, not even to celebrate with others. But Jeremiah thought, *Even if God had not banned me from attending parties, no one would have invited me anyway.* No one wanted to hang out with the guy predicting doom.

Jeremiah looked at the mud creeping over his shins and considered: *All the trouble this prophesying business has caused me would have been worth it if the people had only listened.* Although his messages sometimes drew a crowd, they never drew devotion. He had repeatedly told people how to avoid disaster by repenting of their foolish worship of carved sticks of wood. But did they? No. And now, more than a year since the ferocious Babylonians had besieged Jerusalem, things looked hopeless.

If he had known all that would happen, would he have told God no? Declining the role of prophet was impossible. Even when he tried not to speak God's word, his heart had burned like fire. God's word needed to escape his heart, his mouth—even if it meant more mocking, more hatred.

Jeremiah tried again to pull a foot out of the muck. He couldn't do it. His optimism for a rescue sank, and he prepared to die. Just then someone called his name: "Jeremiah!" It sounded like Ebed-Melech. "Put this rope under your armpits and pad the rope with these old clothes. We're going to pull you out!"

Maybe there was hope after all.

> **KEY VERSE**
>
> For I know the plans I have for you, declares the LORD, plans for welfare and not for evil, to give you a future and a hope. (Jeremiah 29:11)

The start of a new year brings a plethora of awards shows: Grammys, Oscars, Tonys, Golden Globes, Country Music Awards, Pulitzers, and more. We tune in to see who took home a mini gramophone for best song or a statuette for best actress. We often measure success in the number of trophies on the fireplace mantle.

But what if we don't win a blue ribbon for Best in Show? What if no one rewards us for our performance or recognizes our hard work? Jeremiah's life demonstrates that even if no one else celebrates us, God notices our faithfulness.

SETTING THE SCENE

Jeremiah lived at a crucial point in Israel's history. Scripture tells us Jeremiah began his forty-year career as a prophet in the thirteenth year of King Josiah, who reigned 640–609 BC, about three hundred years after the death of David (see Jeremiah 1:2). Many kings, good and bad, had come and gone during those centuries. Josiah was one of the good guys, one of the few kings of whom the Bible declares, "He did what was right in the eyes of the LORD" (2 Kings 22:2).

But before Josiah, Israel had endured two incredibly wicked kings: Manasseh and Amon. Manasseh reigned fifty-five years and "did evil in the eyes of the LORD" (2 Chronicles 33:2). He not only rebuilt the pagan altars that his father, good King Hezekiah, had destroyed, but he erected altars to the foreign gods Baal and Asherah *inside* God's holy temple. He practiced sorcery and witchcraft. And worst of all, he sacrificed his own sons to the false gods.

Later in life, Manasseh repented and removed the pagan altars from the temple, but his son Amon continued the pagan practices. God then declared that He would destroy Jerusalem and "make them a horror to all the kingdoms of the earth because of what Manasseh the son of Hezekiah, king of Judah, did in Jerusalem" (Jeremiah 15:4).

After Manasseh, good King Josiah made many spiritual reforms including repairing the temple. He read God's Word to the people and reinstated the celebration of Passover. It looked like the nation would return to the Lord.

CHRONOLOGY OF JEREMIAH

If you've read the Book of Jeremiah, you may have noticed that it is not written in chronological order. For instance, in Jeremiah 32:1, Jeremiah talks about "the tenth year of Zedekiah king of Judah," but in 36:1, he mentions "the fourth year of Jehoiakim," even though Zedekiah reigned *after* Jehoiakim. So what's going on here? Jeremiah's prophecies are "presented in collections, or 'books.'"[28] To help you understand the sometimes-confusing book, I have arranged the events in Jeremiah's life chronologically here.

SUCCESS TURNED TO FAILURE?

If Jeremiah had thought his gig as prophet would be a long string of successes, his vision of an easy life came crashing down with the death of King Josiah. Josiah's reforms produced only outward change without any transformation of hearts. After the king died in a battle with Egypt, Jeremiah continued to speak to subsequent kings and preached to the people of Judah, but time after time, his words resulted only in his own persecution.

When Jeremiah was in the court of the Lord's house and spoke God's words "I will make this city a curse for all the nations of the earth" (Jeremiah 26:6), the people took hold of him and the priests and other prophets shouted, "You shall die!" (v. 8). The officials of Judah did not view the situation the same way and spared the prophet's life, but the people who were supposed to be God's spokesmen continued to cause trouble for Jeremiah. When Pashhur, a priest in the temple, heard Jeremiah speak God's words of judgment, he responded by beating the prophet and putting him in stocks. There, Jeremiah became "a laughingstock all the day" (Jeremiah 20:7).

No one wanted to hear Jeremiah's words, but they did come true. In 605 BC, Nebuchadnezzar rose to power in Babylon and invaded Judah, taking many of its citizens to Babylon. Nebuchadnezzar installed Jehoiakim, son of Josiah, as king, but Jehoiakim ignored Jeremiah's words too. In fact, at one point when God told Jeremiah to write His words on a scroll, Jehoiakim burned them (Jeremiah 36:23). Jeremiah's words literally went up in smoke.

NO ONE WANTED TO HEAR JEREMIAH'S WORDS, BUT THEY DID COME TRUE.

When Jehoiakim stopped paying the required tribute to Nebuchadnezzar, the Babylonian king returned with his troops, besieged Jerusalem, and took more Judeans—including Jehoiakim—to Babylon. Nebuchadnezzar set up Jehoiakim's brother Zedekiah as a puppet king. Zedekiah "did what was evil in the sight of the LORD his God. He did not humble himself before

Jeremiah the prophet, who spoke from the mouth of the LORD" (2 Chronicles 36:12).

Just when you think Jeremiah's life couldn't get any gloomier, it did. Once, as the prophet tried to leave Jerusalem during a temporary lifting of the siege, soldiers accused him of deserting and put him in a dungeon for many days. Jeremiah appealed to Zedekiah, and the king ordered that Jeremiah be kept instead in the court of the guard. Although not free, he had fresh air and "a loaf of bread was given him daily from the bakers' street, until all the bread of the city was gone" (Jeremiah 37:21).

While in the courtyard, Jeremiah continued to preach God's message, telling everyone that whoever surrendered to the Babylonians would live, but those who stayed in the city would die (Jeremiah 38:2). As you can imagine, this sounded like treason! The Judean officials complained to King Zedekiah that Jeremiah's words were weakening the resolve of the few remaining soldiers. The fickle king allowed the officials to do whatever they wanted to the prophet, and this was how Jeremiah ended up at the bottom of a cistern. Their actions doomed God's spokesman to a slow death of starvation. He survived only because Ebed-Melech, an Ethiopian official in Zedekiah's court, pleaded on his behalf and pulled Jeremiah out.

In 586 BC, King Nebuchadnezzar again attacked Jerusalem, killed Zedekiah, destroyed the temple, and carried still more exiles to Babylon. With all the grief that Jeremiah got from the kings of Israel, you'll be surprised to know that the king of Babylon showed him favor. He allowed Jeremiah to choose whether to go to Babylon, where the king promised to take care of him, or stay in the ruined city of Jerusalem.

Jeremiah chose to stay in Jerusalem. Could things get any worse than living among piles of rubble? They could and did. Some of the remaining Judeans assassinated the Babylonian governor of Judea, and then, fearing retribution from Nebuchadnezzar, they fled to Egypt and took Jeremiah with them—against his will. Tradition tells us his own countrymen stoned him to death there in Egypt because Jeremiah continued to speak against their idolatry. There was no successful ending for the faithful prophet.

BROKEN CISTERNS

Even before Jeremiah found himself sinking in the mud of a broken cistern, God used this type of water-storage vessel as a lesson for the people. In Jeremiah 2:13, God says,

My people have committed two evils:

they have forsaken Me,

the fountain of living waters,

and hewed out cisterns for themselves,

broken cisterns that can hold no water.

People in ancient times built cisterns by digging a hole in the ground to catch rain runoff. Cisterns generally had a bell shape with a narrow opening to slow evaporation, and they had a plaster coating to save every drop of water.[29] In a dry climate, the water from a cistern certainly served its purpose, but it probably did not taste as fresh and pure as water from a spring.

God told the people they had abandoned Him—"the fountain of living waters"—and laboriously tried to dig their own sources of life by crafting man-made idols and religious systems.[30] How often do we do this as well? We reject God's gift of grace and instead try to find success on our own through money, career, or fame. The trouble is, our own efforts always turn out like broken cisterns that hold no water. Our own attempts to find prosperity will always fail. So why not turn to God and drink of His living water?

JEREMIAH'S "SUCCESS"

God gave Jeremiah many messages. In fact, the phrase "Thus says the LORD" appears 150 times in the Book of Jeremiah. Yet God warned the prophet that his message would not be received: "So you shall speak all these words to them, but they will not listen to you. You shall call to them, but they will not answer you" (Jeremiah 7:27).

Perhaps Jeremiah wondered, *How can you go wrong with a sermon directly from the Almighty?* It seemed like a sure thing. Yet no one listened. Jeremiah didn't speak the type of message the people wanted to hear.

Pastor John Nunes writes of Jeremiah:

> His sermons were chock-full of challenging words that got in
> the face and under the skin of those ignoring God's Word. . . .
> These are not the kinds of words that win friends, influence
> people, or satisfy the status quo![31]

Even though Jeremiah had a forty-year career as God's spokesman, did he feel like a success? I doubt it. Yet according to God's standards, Jeremiah was one of the most successful people in history. Jeremiah recorded some of God's own words on success:

> Thus says the LORD:
> "Cursed is the man who trusts in man
>   and makes flesh his strength,
>   whose heart turns away from the LORD.
> He is like a shrub in the desert,
>   and shall not see any good come.
> He shall dwell in the parched places of the wilderness,
>   in an uninhabited salt land.
> "Blessed is the man who trusts in the LORD,
>   whose trust is the LORD.
> He is like a tree planted by water,
>   that sends out its roots by the stream,
> and does not fear when heat comes,
>   for its leaves remain green,
> and is not anxious in the year of drought,
>   for it does not cease to bear fruit." (Jeremiah 17:5–8)

This passage talks about both great prosperity and brutal desolation. The person who trusts in human power and turns away from God will not experience any growth or fruitfulness because he will live alone in a dusty, drought-ridden desert. The Judeans who refused to listen to Jeremiah illustrated this. They trusted in their armies to save them, in their own abilities to get themselves out of trouble, and in foreign powers to protect them. As a result, the nation was broken and defeated.

LISTEN TO GOD'S DEFINITION OF SUCCESS: "BLESSED IS THE MAN WHO TRUSTS IN THE LORD" (JEREMIAH 17:7).

But listen to God's definition of success: "Blessed is the man who trusts in the LORD" (Jeremiah 17:7). The Hebrew word for "bless," *barak,* means "to bestow ability for success."[32] Certainly Jeremiah exemplified "the man who trusts in the LORD." And although he didn't receive accolades, Jeremiah continued to bear fruit in his forty-year ministry to God's people, and his words speak to us today, 2,400 years later. I believe the Lord saw Jeremiah as a tree firmly planted in the soil of divine love that continually produced the fruit of obedience.

ANOTHER STORY OF SUCCESSFUL OBEDIENCE

When I read about Jeremiah's life, I think of a more personal story— that of my own husband. Like Jeremiah, John has served in ministry for about forty years. His intelligence, wit, and caring nature seemed to guarantee astounding success. And yet . . .

Well, I'll let him tell you his story:

> In early January 1977, I announced to my family and teachers at the University of Wisconsin—Green Bay that a long night of prayer led me to change my plans from pursuing the riches of a career in the law to becoming a minister of the Gospel. "What a bleepingly stupid waste of a life," opined one professor who hoped my talents would lead elsewhere. Confident in my calling, I graduated college summa cum laude in three years and never really looked back. Classes, field work, and vicarage all went well at the seminary. After I passed my theological interview, one of my seminary professors wished me

Godspeed with "May you be well used by the Lord." So I set off for a life of service in "the real world," certain that I would be well used by the Lord.

Fast-forward forty years. My wife and I had recently discussed how this world's evaluation of success and failure is often at odds with God's purposes. Without excuses, self-pity, pandering for compliments, or pious posturing, I own up to the decline of the church I have served for decades. It is one thing to believe that only the Holy Spirit can convert anyone and provide real church growth. It is another to know God promises to build His Church and yet have every quantifiable number (humanly speaking) go south. Personifying the line "We feebly struggle, they in glory shine" (*LSB* 677:4) can put one on a roller coaster between despairing or sharpening our focus on "His strength made perfect in our weakness."

While in and out of the seminary, I served developmentally disabled people, the indigent, and senior citizens in northern Wisconsin and interned in a hearing church with a deaf ministry. I served as campus chaplain, ministered to deaf people in the western third of Montana, and became assistant pastor to some of the nicest people on the planet. When my vicarage congregation called me to serve as its pastor, the move brought us much closer geographically to family. It also presented some unique challenges: a congregation so strapped for resources that it was twenty-four months behind on its mortgage; deaf ministry with decreasing district support; the church's prior commitment to mainstream forty-five developmentally disabled adults into a congregation with barely twice that many total members; a swiftly changing neighborhood with increasing unemployment, gang violence, crime, and "white flight"; and the nationwide challenge of a post-Christian culture. The God who created the universe by the power of His Word is more than capable of handling all of those obstacles, and the God who died to save His lost and fallen creation certainly has the motivation to do so. But the numbers . . .

Some parishioners who moved twenty-five, forty, even sixty miles away still drove in regularly for worship, but the members who moved to other states could only return for annual family visits. In light of the recessions of 2001 and 2008, what could a congregation that never reached "critical mass" do? And where is God when dedicated service, faithfulness to His Word, and love for His mission to reach the lost and disciple the saved sees many called but few chosen?

With the resources we do have, we built an addition onto our church, opened and staffed an afterschool outreach to our community, provided worship space for a Pakistani and two separate Hispanic ministries, conducted an outreach to Middle Eastern Muslims, and sent two men to the seminary. I continue to provide spiritual care for our deaf members, help provide pastoral care for a neighboring congregation, support local and national missions, model sacrificial stewardship of time, talents, and treasures, and encourage my wife's writing, speaking, and singing, which have reached thousands of people.

The ultimate fruitfulness of all our labors is totally in Jesus' nail-scarred hands. Some days we will revel in the "victories" God allows us to see. Other days we will probably bemoan God's tardiness in maturing the seeds we are sowing. While we have breath, we will continue to explore ways to share the bad news of God's Law and the great Good News of the Gospel of Jesus Christ.

Although the numbers of people in the pews of our church may not impress a lot of people, John's caring heart has ministered to many. The people of our congregation often comment that his sermons speak directly to their needs. And whenever I attend a funeral of a member who experienced a long illness, the family never fails to express gratitude for John's caring heart. He faithfully visits people struggling with health problems, helping them connect with God, see their value in Christ, and maybe find something to smile about. Perhaps this talent hasn't earned medals, but I am certain God sees John's compassion and faithfulness.

OBJECT LESSONS

My husband often uses object lessons in his sermons, especially when speaking to children. Jeremiah used a similar approach. He filled his messages with visuals that captured the people's attention.

A Linen Loincloth (Jeremiah 13:1–11). How strange is this? God told Jeremiah to bury his underwear! He instructed Jeremiah to buy a linen loincloth, wear it around his waist, and then hide it under a rock at the Euphrates River. After many days, God told him to get the loincloth from under the rock; of course, it was ruined. The loincloth, which was worn close to the skin, symbolized Israel, who had once clung to the Lord but now had experienced spiritual decay.

Potter's Clay (Jeremiah 18:1–17). The Lord instructed Jeremiah to go to the potter's house. The prophet observed the potter working at the wheel, forming a pot. When the vessel the potter worked on became spoiled, he reworked it into something new. God said that just like the potter had the right to destroy his original work, God had the right to destroy the nation He had formed but which now had become evil.

Broken Clay Jars (Jeremiah 19:1–12). God demonstrated His coming judgment by having Jeremiah break a piece of pottery in the valley where the people had sacrificed their children to foreign gods. Just as Jeremiah broke the flask, God would break and destroy Jerusalem.

Two Baskets of Figs (Jeremiah 24:1–10). God gave Jeremiah a vision of two baskets of figs. One held perfectly ripe figs while the other contained rotten figs that couldn't be eaten. God told Jeremiah He would regard the Judean exiles who went to Babylon as the good figs. The Lord would build them up and bring them back. But the people who remained—proud and un-repentant—would be destroyed like spoiled figs.

Yoke (Jeremiah 27:2–15). Here "Jeremiah used a visual aid to demonstrate the futility of joining other nations in resistance to Babylon."[33] Because God had decided to use Nebuchad-nezzar in His divine plan, every nation needed to "put its neck under the yoke of the king of Babylon" (v. 8).

A Field (Jeremiah 32:1–15). While Jeremiah was imprisoned in the courtyard of the guard, God told him to buy a field from his cousin in his hometown of Anathoth. Practically speaking, this made no sense because Jerusalem was under Babylonian siege and Anathoth was occupied by foreign soldiers. But this act gave the people hope that "houses and fields and vineyards shall again be bought in this land" (v. 15).

WHEN YOU FEEL LIKE A PROFESSIONAL FAILURE

Jeremiah lived an exemplary life. He accepted God's call to a career in ministry that became a life of rejection and persecution. Although he faithfully followed and obeyed Yahweh, I doubt anyone but God would have described him as successful. Yet as we have seen, Jeremiah lived a life God defined as "blessed." His trust in almighty God gave him success in the spiritual realm and made his life incredibly fruitful in God's kingdom.

So what can we learn about success from Jeremiah's life?

God often calls us to a job where we feel we will fail, but He equips us for the task. In the first chapter of Jeremiah, we learn how God called him to be a prophet:

Now the word of the LORD came to me, saying,
    "Before I formed you in the womb I knew you,

69

and before you were born I consecrated you;
I appointed you a prophet to the nations." (Jeremiah 1:4–5)

Even before Jeremiah was born, God had a specific assignment for him, and He has a purpose for your life too. Paul writes in Ephesians, "We are His workmanship, created in Christ Jesus for good works, which God prepared beforehand, that we should walk in them" (Ephesians 2:10). God did not single out only Jeremiah; He designed you for a particular calling as well.

Jeremiah did not immediately accept the job. He protested, "Ah, Lord GOD! Behold, I do not know how to speak, for I am only a youth" (Jeremiah 1:6). But God didn't take no for an answer. The Lord promised to equip Jeremiah for the assignment with His constant presence and His very own words.

Success in God's kingdom doesn't depend on our own abilities. We don't need a commanding stage presence, amazing intellect, or stellar marketing skills. God gives what we need to complete the work He puts in front of us.

Eugene Peterson writes,

> God does not send us into the dangerous and exacting life of faith because we are qualified; he chooses us in order to qualify us for what he wants us to be and do.[34]

STEP INTO WHATEVER ROLE GOD HAS FOR YOU, WHETHER YOU FEEL CAPABLE OR NOT.

Step into whatever role God has for you, whether or not you feel capable. Serve in the armed forces or parent toddlers. Care for an elderly parent or lead a corporation. Before you were born, God picked you for a specific purpose. You might tell God you can't deal with complex problems or change one more dirty diaper. But as His baptized daughter, the Lord promises to walk beside you and give you what you need for success—smack-dab in your messy life.

God has plans to prosper us, but that prosperity may not look like what we expect. One of the most quoted verses from all of Scripture comes from Jeremiah:

> For I know the plans I have for you, declares the LORD, plans for welfare and not for evil, to give you a future and a hope. (Jeremiah 29:11)

Perhaps we love this verse because it sounds like God has outlined plans for worldly success. Other versions present this verse as including God's "plans for prosperity" (NASB) and His announcement "I want you to enjoy success" (NIRV). Such versions can lead to the message we hear from certain preachers dispensing a "prosperity gospel" that proclaims God intends us to have nothing but wealth, comfort, and perfect health.

But let's take a look at the context of this verse. Those oft-quoted words come in the middle of a long letter Jeremiah wrote to exiles in Babylon. Think about that for a moment. The people who received the message of God's plans for prosperity had been ripped from their homes and relocated to a country 1,600 miles away where they didn't know the language or understand the culture.

In the letter, Jeremiah told the exiles to "build houses and live in them; plant gardens and eat their produce" (Jeremiah 29:5) because God had declared that their time in Babylon would continue for seventy years. An exile of seven decades meant most of the adults who heard Jeremiah's message would never see their homeland again.

Yet right after God gave bad news about the long exile, He said, "I plan to prosper you." How do we make sense of this?

First, let's look at the word translated in this verse as "welfare," "prosper," or "success." The Hebrew word *salam* is often rendered as "peace," but also as "well-being," "health," "completeness," and "safety." It carries the idea of wholeness and the absence of strife.[35] This kind of prosperity isn't wealth; rather, God gives us the prize of serenity in our souls that can't be quantified or measured.

Second, let's examine what comes after that famous verse:

> Then you will call upon Me and come and pray to Me, and I
> will hear you. You will seek Me and find Me, when you seek
> Me with all your heart. (Jeremiah 29:12–13)

God's plans for welfare and wholeness have nothing to do with luxury cruises or designer handbags. His idea of peace and prosperity is the soul that seeks Him wholeheartedly, the mouth that calls out to Him in prayer. He guarantees that when we seek Him, we find Him, and in Him we have all we need.

God doesn't measure success in the number of trophies or the size of our audience. He uses the measuring tape of faithfulness. If our world handed out trophies for faithfulness and obedience, Jeremiah would be in the running. Nothing deterred the prophet from the life to which God called him; nothing changed the message God gave him to speak. He might have experienced more positive attention if he had preached, "Peace, peace," like some of Judah's other prophets (Jeremiah 8:11), or promised a two-year exile like the more popular prophet Hananiah (Jeremiah 28:11). But he obeyed the Lord, who had instructed him to let His words change the people instead of allowing the people to change His words (Jeremiah 15:19).

I love Jeremiah's story because I think we tend to believe that when God calls us to a task, everything will go smoothly. God asks you to teach a Bible study? Surely the chairs around the table will fill immediately. You feel called to witness to a neighbor? The grouchy person next door will instantly want to know Jesus. Called to youth ministry? Your church's high school group will surely grow in numbers and devotion.

Of course, sometimes this happens, and we praise God when it does. But when life doesn't turn out the way we expected, we might assume we heard God wrong. Maybe He didn't want me to write that book, take that leadership position, start a new ministry at my church. Jeremiah's life tells us that even when we clearly hear God's call and obey, we might not experience the kind of success the world applauds.

God's Measure of Success

At the beginning of Jeremiah's career as prophet, God commanded him, "Say to them everything that I command you" (Jeremiah 1:17). But in the next breath He warns, "They will fight against you" (v. 19). There would be no thunderous applause, no red carpets, no award ceremonies. Yet Jeremiah obeyed.

> LET'S NOT MEASURE OUR SUCCESS BY HOW MANY PEOPLE HONOR US, OR GAUGE OUR FAILURE BY HOW MANY PEOPLE REJECT US. MAY GOD'S APPROVAL BE THE ONLY RECOGNITION WE NEED.

May we follow the example of Jeremiah even if no one follows us on Instagram. May we live out God's calling in our lives even if no one calls out our name at an awards ceremony. May we stand firm in faithfulness to the Lord even if we never receive a standing ovation.

Let's not measure our success by how many people honor us, or gauge our failure by how many people reject us. May God's approval be the only recognition we need.

CHAPTER 5

JOHN THE BAPTIST: PECULIAR PREACHER

TIMELINE

Joseph	1915 BC
Rahab	1406 BC
David	1010 BC
Jeremiah	628 BC
John the Baptist	1st Century AD

John looked at the line of people forming. Fewer people than last month, but still a sizable number. People hungry for God—for a right relationship with Yahweh.

John looked down at himself and laughed. Who would have thought anyone would come to see this? A man dressed in a coarse camel's-hair coat tied with a leather belt. Usually people were drawn by opulence, not poverty. Yet he had no doubt about why his message drew hundreds: He continually pointed the way to the coming Savior. He told all who

Map © iStock / Peter Hermes Furian

would listen that he was merely a voice crying in the wilderness to prepare the way of the Lord.

People had grown tired of religious hypocrisy. Pharisees and Sadducees strutting in their long, flowing robes, imposing greater and greater burdens of regulations. The people hungered for truth.

So when John began preaching in the wilderness, they came. Though the journey to the desert involved some hardship, they came. Though his message of repentance might have hurt their pride, they came. Hundreds arrived to confess their sins, become right with God, and receive Baptism.

Even some of the religious elite came—though probably only out of curiosity or to check out their competition. They asked John, "Who are you?" Knowing that they might wonder if he was the Messiah, he adamantly stated he wasn't. "I'm not Elijah. Or the Prophet. I'm here to prepare the way for the Christ."

Then one day, John saw the One the world was waiting for. As he stood in the Jordan River with the sun sparkling on the water, John had just baptized one man and looked toward the next person in line when he saw it was Jesus. Humbled, John protested that Jesus should baptize him instead, but Jesus insisted and stepped into the river.

Now, days later, as John turned his attention to the small crowd, one of his followers said, "Rabbi, the man you were with across the Jordan? The One you pointed out? Everyone is going to Him!" Clearly this loyal disciple of John felt distraught that someone else was drawing the attention John had been receiving.

But John knew—this was the way it was supposed to be. He put his hand on his friend's shoulder and said, "Listen, you have heard me say many times that I am not the Christ. I am only the one sent ahead to prepare the way. Now He has come! He must become greater, and I must become less and less."

John then stepped into the river and called for the next person desiring Baptism. He still had work to do.

> ### KEY VERSE
> He must increase, but I must decrease. (John 3:30)

It's not easy, opening for a rock band. The crowd has paid to see the headline act and doesn't care about the music of the second-best. The warm-up band gains exposure by playing before the audience, but its members can't wait until they're the stars.

John the Baptist, however, didn't despise his part as the warm-up band for the Messiah. Even though people flocked to hear his message, he knew the spotlight wasn't meant for him. John embraced his lower position as Jesus became the headline act.

SETTING THE SCENE

In the previous chapter, we witnessed the fall of Jerusalem. Jeremiah had warned the people and cautioned their rulers, but they refused to repent. Israel experienced horrific defeat when King Nebuchadnezzar broke through Jerusalem's walls and destroyed the temple in 587 BC. He took most of Jerusalem's citizens to Babylon and left only the poorest people behind.

We learned about Jeremiah's letter to the exiles in Babylon, in which he urged them to build houses, plant gardens, marry, and have children because their separation from their homeland would last seventy years (Jeremiah 29:5–6). The prophet even foretold of God's plan to destroy Babylon at the end of those seven decades (Jeremiah 25:12–14). Although Jeremiah didn't live to see this prophecy come true, the Persian emperor Cyrus the Great defeated the Babylonians in 539 BC. A year later, he allowed some of the Judean exiles to return to their homeland. By 516 BC, they had rebuilt the temple, and in 445 BC, Nehemiah led the work of rebuilding the city walls. Life resumed in Jerusalem.

But life never returned to the splendor of the days of King David and King Solomon. For the next four hundred years, the people of Israel lived under the reign of many foreign rulers including the Greeks and Romans. And although worship at the temple continued, no new prophets appeared after Malachi, who wrote his message in 430 BC.

A Prophetic Success?

EVEN BEFORE JOHN ARRIVED IN THE WORLD, HE DREW A LOT OF ATTENTION.

So you can imagine the excitement when, in AD 29, people heard about the preacher in the Judean wilderness who wore clothes made of camel's hair and lived off locusts and wild honey. His wardrobe sounded reminiscent of the prophet Elijah (2 Kings 1:8), so people flocked to hear the words of this man, John the Baptist. They hungered for a fresh word from God.

Even before John arrived in the world, he drew a lot of attention. His story began when his father, Zechariah, an aging priest, received the honor of burning incense in the temple. Because Israel had approximately twenty thousand priests at that time, each priest likely received this privilege only once in his lifetime. Zechariah had waited a long time for this, and God chose to make that moment even more spectacular for Zechariah by sending an angel with an announcement:

> Do not be afraid, Zechariah, for your prayer has been heard, and your wife Elizabeth will bear you a son, and you shall call his name John. And you will have joy and gladness, and many will rejoice at his birth, for he will be great before the Lord. And he must not drink wine or strong drink, and he will be filled with the Holy Spirit, even from his mother's womb. And he will turn many of the children of Israel to the Lord their God, and he will go before Him in the spirit and power of Elijah, to turn the hearts of the fathers to the children, and the disobedient to the wisdom of the just, to make ready for the Lord a people prepared. (Luke 1:13–17)

Unfortunately, Zechariah couldn't fathom all this: *Elizabeth and I will have a child now? At our ages?* Because he expressed doubt, he lost the ability to speak for the next nine months. During that silent period, he probably thought a lot about what the angel had said and wondered how it would all play out: *Our son will be great before the Lord? God will fill him with His Holy Spirit? Our son will turn hearts to the Lord? He will work in the spirit of Elijah?*

I imagine the prophecy that truly sent his heart racing was the last one: his son would prepare people for the coming of the Lord. *Does that mean the Messiah will soon arrive?*

The priest and his wife surely rejoiced with the confirmation of the last prediction when their young cousin Mary arrived for an extended visit. When Mary greeted Elizabeth, Elizabeth's "baby leaped in her womb" (Luke 1:41). Elizabeth's unborn son—already filled with the Holy Spirit—confirmed that the baby in Mary's womb was the Christ.

When Zechariah and Elizabeth's baby arrived, they had the usual celebration on the eighth day for the circumcision. Certainly everyone present rejoiced with this couple who had long given up on the joy of having a child. And perhaps they suspected something special from the baby born to a mother past childbearing age. We know they puzzled over Elizabeth's insistence on naming the baby John even though no relatives had that name. And they marveled when Zechariah suddenly regained his ability to talk as he decisively wrote on a tablet, "His name is John."

These startling events became the talk of the hill country in Judea, and everyone wondered, "What then will this child be?" (Luke 1:66). Perhaps they pictured this little one becoming an important government official or a powerful priest in the temple.

I doubt any of them expected John to be a wild man living in the desert.

Yet Scripture tells us this is where John took up residence. Luke 1:80 says, "And the child grew and became strong in spirit, and he was in the wilderness until the day of his public appearance to Israel." It seems fitting

THIS ROUGH-LOOK-
ING MAN HAD NO
POLITICAL POWER,
NO AUTHORITY IN
RELIGIOUS CIRCLES,
YET PEOPLE CRAVED
HIS MESSAGE BE-
CAUSE HE SPOKE
TRUTH.

that John spent a lot of time in the wilderness—a location that often served "as a place
of spiritual formation and testing in God's
presence."[36]

Because Zechariah and Elizabeth were
already "advanced in years" (Luke 1:18) when
John was born, they probably did not live to
see his ministry. Don't you wonder if some of
their neighbors shook their heads when they
heard that the much-talked-about child had

CAMEL'S-HAIR CLOTHES
AND WEIRD BUGS

Now John wore a garment of camel's hair and a leather belt
around his waist, and his food was locusts and wild honey.
(Matthew 3:4)

John did not dress to impress. Unlike the religious leaders of the day who liked to walk around in flowing robes (Mark
12:38), John adopted the wardrobe of a prophet much like Elijah
(2 Kings 1:8). Goat or camel hair could be woven into a thick
cloth that was practically waterproof and all but impervious to
weather. This cloth could also stand as a symbol of grief and
mourning, which suited John's message of repentance and sor-
row over sin.

John also set himself apart by his diet, the food of the desert: locusts and wild honey. Locusts were an important source
of protein. Desert people would collect them, remove their legs,
dry them, and grind them into flour. (At least they didn't have to
swallow those spiny bodies and prickly legs!) John might have
mixed the flour with the honey. His unusual lifestyle reinforced
his unique message.[37]

taken up wearing camel's-hair outfits and eating bugs? Can't you see them whispering, "It's a good thing Zechariah and Elizabeth didn't live to see this!"

Yet people from all over Judea, the Jordan Valley, and Jerusalem came to hear this unusual character. A few probably came to see the unique wardrobe choices, but they stayed for the message. John, like so many Old Testament prophets, preached a message of repentance. And when the people confessed their sins, John baptized them.

This rough-looking man had no political power, no authority in religious circles, yet people craved his message because he spoke Yahweh's truth. They felt the burden of their sins and longed for release.

Success in Pointing to Jesus

Even though hundreds of people crowded around John, he pointed away from himself and to the coming Messiah. When people asked John if he might be the Christ, he said, "I baptize you with water, but He who is mightier than I is coming, the strap of whose sandals I am not worthy to untie. He will baptize you with the Holy Spirit and fire" (Luke 3:16).

Then one day, while John was baptizing at the Jordan River, Jesus showed up and asked John to baptize Him. John protested, "I need to be baptized by You, and do You come to me?" (Matthew 3:14). Jesus insisted, and when He came up out of the water, John witnessed the sign that God had promised would signify the Messiah (John 1:32–34). The heavens opened and the Spirit descended on Jesus like a dove. A voice from heaven said, "This is My beloved Son, with whom I am well pleased" (Matthew 3:17). That dispelled all doubts. Now John was certain that Jesus was the Christ (John 1:32–34). When John saw Jesus, he said, "Behold, the Lamb of God, who takes away the sin of the world!" (John 1:29).

John's Questions

But John was human. At times, he experienced doubt—especially while in prison.

JOHN'S BAPTISM

Zechariah and Elizabeth's son was called "the Baptist" because of his practice of baptizing the people who came to him and confessed their sins.

Even before John performed Baptisms, some Jewish groups used a baptism ritual, especially for Gentiles wanting to convert to Judaism. Proselytes needed to renounce worship of idols and heathen superstitions.[38] After promising to obey the Law of Moses, they underwent circumcision, and the baptism completed their acceptance into the Jewish community.[39] However, John upset the religious elite because he "insisted that Jews needed to repent and be baptized, implying that they were no better than Gentiles."[40]

John the Baptist distinguished between the Baptism he administered and the one Jesus would provide, saying, "I baptize you with water for repentance, but He who is coming after me is mightier than I, whose sandals I am not worthy to carry. He will baptize you with the Holy Spirit and fire" (Matthew 3:11). John's Baptism with water demonstrated repentance and prepared a person to receive the message of Christ. However, when Jesus baptizes with the Holy Spirit, people receive forgiveness of sins and the Spirit's transforming power. "Christ is the one who brings the power to Holy Baptism and makes us forever clean from sin."[41]

Jesus even submitted to John's Baptism. Luther wrote that Jesus did this "becoming a sinner for us, taking upon [H]imself the sins which [H]e had not committed, and wiping them out and drowning them in [H]is holy baptism."[42]

Herod Agrippa (son of Herod the Great and tetrarch of Galilee and Perea) knew of John the Baptist and feared him because John spoke the truth about his marriage to Herodias. Herod Agrippa had first married the daughter of Aretus IV, ruler of neighboring Nabataea. Then he fell in love with Herodias—his niece who was married to his stepbrother Philip. Herodias agreed to Herod Agrippa's marriage proposal, but only on the condition that he divorce his first wife. John the Baptist openly spoke against this marriage, which went against Levitical law (Leviticus 20:21).[43]

According to the Jewish historian Josephus, Herod imprisoned John in his fortress Machaerus in Perea on the east side of the Jordan.[44] Although he might have preferred to simply do away with John, Herod feared public opinion, which stood on the side of the prophet. Imprisoning John the Baptist kept him from publicly denouncing Herod and appeased Herodias (Matthew 14:1–5).

While in prison, it appears that John felt uncertain. We know John sent two of his disciples to ask Jesus, "Are You the one who is to come, or shall we look for another?" (Luke 7:19). Because John had previously given such a sure confession of Jesus as Messiah after seeing the Spirit descend on Him like a dove, some commentators think John sent his followers so they would be assured about Jesus.[45] But John was as human as we are, so we can understand how doubt and depression could emerge as he sat in a dungeon. Another commentator writes, "Most likely, John is concerned because his present experience does not match the message he gave about the Coming One's arrival, which promised blessing on those who repent and judgment on those who do not."[46] The prophet had preached a message of judgment, and Jesus didn't live up to John's image of a judge.

In any case, Jesus didn't rebuke John for his doubts. He simply told John's disciples, "Go and tell John what you have seen and heard" (Luke 7:22). Jesus pointed to His mighty works as fulfilled prophecies: the blind see, the deaf hear, and the lame walk (Isaiah 35:5–6). The dead are raised (Isaiah 26:19), and the poor hear good news preached (Isaiah 61:1).

When Jesus cited the verse about the poor, John must have wondered why Jesus didn't include the rest of it: "to proclaim liberty to the captives, and the opening of the prison to those who are bound" (Isaiah 61:1). If Jesus was the Messiah, why was John in prison? Even though he accepted his "success" as the warm-up band to the main event, I imagine he saw no purpose in being imprisoned without the freedom to point others to Jesus. God's ways must have baffled him.

In the end, John died a horrific death at the command of his nemesis, Herodias. Herod gave himself a birthday party and invited all the government officials and leading citizens of Galilee. Herodias's daughter entertained the guests with a sensual dance. Herod, so taken with the girl, promised her anything she wanted. The girl ran to her mother to get input on what to ask for, and Herodias saw her chance: "Ask for the head of John the Baptist on a platter." Herod regretted his promise but fulfilled it for fear of looking foolish in front of his guests. He sent an executioner to the prison, who beheaded John and delivered the head on a tray. When John's disciples heard what had happened, they came to get his body and bury it.

WHEN YOU FEEL SECOND-BEST

John the Baptist is unique in history as the last Old Testament prophet. He certainly portrayed a distinctive figure, dressing in odd clothes, eating strange foods. But this prophet had no goal of distinction—his message of repentance was to prepare people for the long-awaited Messiah. What can we learn about success from this unique man?

At the beginning of this chapter, we looked at an incident from John's life when some of his disciples became concerned that the newcomer, Jesus, was stealing John's thunder. Now let's read this story in Scripture:

> And they came to John and said to him, "Rabbi, He who was with you across the Jordan, to whom you bore witness—look, He is baptizing, and all are going to Him." John answered, "A person cannot receive even one thing unless it is given him from heaven. You yourselves bear me witness, that I said, 'I am not the Christ, but I have been sent before Him.' The one who has the bride is the bridegroom. The friend of the bridegroom, who stands and hears him, rejoices greatly at the bridegroom's voice. Therefore this joy of mine is now complete. He must increase, but I must decrease." (John 3:26–30)

John's disciples were concerned that Jesus had more followers. But John had no fear of losing fame or reputation. This passage teaches us three lessons about success.

Any success we have comes from God. John wasn't the type that usually drew crowds. He didn't hold a powerful political position. He wasn't an influential religious figure. Yet he upstaged the political and religious leaders of the day, and he did it by telling people a message that normally didn't attract the masses: they needed to repent and change.

Jesus pointed this out when He talked to the crowds about John:

> What did you go out into the wilderness to see? A reed shaken by the wind? What then did you go out to see? A man dressed in soft clothing? Behold, those who wear soft clothing are in kings' houses. What then did you go out to see? A prophet? Yes, I tell you, and more than a prophet. (Matthew 11:7–9)

The people didn't go to the Jordan River for the scenery. They didn't crowd around John to see a fashion show. John didn't achieve success because he followed trends or courted popular opinion.

Yet hundreds of people came to hear him—the first prophet God had sent in four hundred years—because they hungered to hear from Yahweh. John knew that any success he had in terms of numbers came not because of a flashy appearance or flattering message. He realized any achievements he accomplished came as a gift of God. Paul E. Kretzmann writes in his commentary:

> If any man does anything in the kingdom of God, that is the blessing of God. It is not like in the field of human endeavor, where each person selects the work that suits him best, and then expects results in proportion to the labor and ability expended. In the work of the Kingdom God alone gives the increase.[47]

JOHN THE BAPTIST REALIZED ANY ACHIEVEMENTS HE ACCOMPLISHED CAME AS A GIFT OF GOD.

Like John, we may experience some success in numbers. We may receive a raise in salary or see a dramatic increase in attendance at the Bible study we lead. It's tempting to take the credit, but let's take John's words to heart—a person cannot receive even one thing unless it's given to him by God.

Success comes as we embrace our God-given roles. From the very beginning of John's ministry, he knew his place in history. His mission was that of a courier announcing the coming of an important King so all roads could be prepared, all potholes removed.[48] John exhibited extreme humility when he insisted he was not even worthy to carry Jesus' sandals (Matthew 3:11), a job of the lowest slave in the household. John's view of himself wasn't negatively skewed; he knew Christ's identity as Messiah, and he understood his own identity as the herald.

Going back to our passage in John 3, John the Baptist presents another picture: "The one who has the bride is the bridegroom. The friend of the bridegroom, who stands and hears him, rejoices greatly at the bridegroom's voice. Therefore this joy of mine is now complete" (John 3:29). Jesus was the Bridegroom, the One who has the bride. John embraced his role as the friend who rejoiced in the sound of the Bridegroom's voice. He felt nothing but pure joy in his role in the wedding party.

John's acceptance of his role inspires me. I cringe at the thought of how I have often tried to steal the spotlight. One incident from high school stands out. Every year my school presented a pop concert. Choirs, small groups, and soloists sang arrangements of oldies and songs from the Top 40. One year, two of my friends worked up an arrangement of "Making Our Dreams Come True" from the TV sitcom *Laverne and Shirley*. To include me, they graciously asked me to play the tambourine with the back-up band. I should have been content to stand in the background and enjoy their fantastic performance. But the bright stage lights turned my usually introverted self into some kind of upstaging maniac. I banged the tambourine on my hip. I waved it above my head. I flipped my ponytail. And when

I got laughs from the audience, I played it up even more. I stole the moment from my talented friends.

Whenever we humans get a taste of importance, prestige, or fame, we tend to want more. Elected to vice president of our service club, we look at the attention the president gets and set our sights on that position. Promotion in our company leads us to race our colleagues to the next rung on the corporate ladder. Moms look at successes of the children of their friends and start to push their own kids to do more. Seldom do we experience satisfaction when we look toward our standing in the world instead of toward the vocations God has given us.

> LET'S NOT STRIVE FOR THE SPOTLIGHT, BUT AIM IT ON JESUS.

John the Baptist accepted his role as the warm-up band, the messenger announcing the King, the Bridegroom's friend. Let's follow his example and embrace the roles God has given us. Let's not strive for the spotlight, but aim it on Jesus.

JESUS AFFIRMED JOHN'S GREATNESS

John the Baptist continually exhibited humility, but Jesus noticed His cousin's importance. He told the people, "I tell you, among those born of women none is greater than John" (Luke 7:28a). However, Jesus continued with a puzzling statement: "Yet the one who is least in the kingdom of God is greater than he" (v. 28b). What did He mean by that? Jesus acknowledged that no one had fulfilled his calling any better than John. Yet John lived at the conclusion of Old Testament times. He did not experience Jesus' triumph over sin and death and the coming of the kingdom of God. Because we live after the resurrection, we each have greater knowledge of God's plan through the gift of the Holy Spirit.

Success is becoming less so Jesus can become more. John the Baptist's well-known line "He must increase, but I must decrease" (John 3:30) is easy to say but not to live. Yes, John had already displayed his humility when he compared himself to the lowest household slave, but picture yourself in John's sandals. You have a ministry reaching hundreds of people who come from miles around to hear *you* preach and to receive Baptism from *your* hand. You see lives transformed. It all might go to your head. When Jesus comes, you know any renown you experience must now shift to Him—but can you give it up?

John the Baptist passed the test. He never claimed the limelight for himself. He purposefully sought to become less so Jesus could become greater. John saw his true position in relation to the Son of God and never looked for more than what he had been given. "When we truly understand who Christ is, our pride and self-importance melt away."[49]

In this world where so many seek more Instagram followers, greater name recognition, and more attention at work, what does becoming less look like?

When I think of becoming less, I think of Ken Baisden, a pastor I met years ago. Before this man served the Lord in the ministry, he served our country in the military. He flew B-52 bombers for the United States Air Force, even receiving the Distinguished Flying Cross for successfully landing a crippled B-52 that had suffered complete electrical failure in flight. With a blackout cockpit, all gyros and heading information inoperative, and no airspeed indicators, Ken successfully dove the plane twenty thousand feet in total darkness to land on an unlit runway with no lights on the aircraft. Few people possess this level of skill.

However, during one of his missions in a B-47, the plane went out of control and started rolling. He and the other pilot used their ejection seats to literally "blow" them up and out of the aircraft, which spiraled downward at nearly 500 mph. Baisden's ejection seat tore through his parachute canopy, leaving him with a little over half of the chute's panels and a rapid descent from sixteen thousand feet—more than three miles! As he was falling, he saw he was headed for a bunch of enormous boulders and prayed, "Thank You, Lord, for a good life. Thank You for a good wife. Amen." As he looked at the ground getting closer, he added, "It looks like I'll see You in about two minutes. Amen." He landed in a hundred-foot-tall tree, taking out two branches (later measured at 33 feet long and a foot in diameter), which saved his life. Incredibly, he never hit the ground. The fall resulted in several spinal compressions, severely injured knees, damaged hips, and shock.

When he eventually healed from his injuries, Lt. Baisden could have had his pick of professions. His commanding officer, himself en route to becoming a three-star general, encouraged Ken to stay in the service and promised accelerated promotions to the rank of brigadier general. Alternatively, Baisden could have transferred to the aircraft industry. High-ranking officials of both Boeing and McDonnell Douglas had promised to utilize his skills when he left the military. But after twenty years of service to our country, Ken Baisden decided to go into the ministry, citing the respect he had always had for the pastors in his life. After graduating from the seminary, he led four different churches in Texas and one in Arizona before taking a call to serve at a residential home for developmentally disabled adults in Aurora, Illinois.

This home was situated across the street from our church, and some of its residents attended our services. Because of this, my husband knew Pastor Baisden, and he remembers clearly the first time he met this humble man. My husband, John, was leading devotions for some of the residents at the home when he noticed Pastor Baisden walk in at a side door. A few minutes later, one of the residents sneezed a sneeze of mythic proportions. Pastor Baisden pulled out his own handkerchief and cleaned up the mess. Although the sneeze could have been the result of a cold or the flu, Pastor Baisden jumped right in without thought for his own health. His job description did not include cleaning up bodily fluids, but he didn't hesitate to help.

Pastor Baisden embraced his role at this facility where the people had no knowledge of his high-flying career as a pilot. They didn't care about his medals. They only knew that he loved them and cared about them. One of the things he did for them was to develop a visual catechism that enabled

> WHEN WE LIVE TO GLORIFY JESUS, WE DON'T MIND BECOMING THE WARM-UP BAND OR THE BACKUP SINGERS.

residents with low verbal abilities to learn and communicate about spiritual matters.

Instead of flying high, Pastor Baisden chose to stoop low. Instead of stepping up to a career where people would salute him wherever he went, he chose to work with people who needed help with the most basic tasks. Instead of opting for a life of financial gain, he chose a life of humble service. Pastor Baisden became less so that others could see Jesus more.

God's Measure of Success

This world continually tells us we need to reach for the stars, but Pastor Baisden chose a lower position. Everyone around us searches for the spotlight to stand in, but John the Baptist strove to work behind the Star. We hear that we should stop at nothing and stay hungry for success, but a true Christ follower tries to get out of the way and simply point to Jesus.

John the Baptist defined success as becoming less instead of more. When we live to glorify Jesus, we don't mind becoming the warm-up band or the backup singers.

CHAPTER 6

THE SAMARITAN WOMAN: FIVE-TIME FAILURE

TIMELINE

Joseph	1915 BC
Rahab	1406 BC
David	1010 BC
Jeremiah	628 BC
John the Baptist	1st Century AD
Samaritan Woman	1st Century AD

My water jar perched on my head, I made my way to the town well. As I neared the stone structure surrounding the life-giving source of water, I couldn't help but think of what had happened there only a few days ago.

I had gone to the well at noon. Most of my neighbors went in the cool morning hours, but I preferred to go when no one else was there. My heart sank when I saw a man sitting near the well. *Is this someone else who will ridicule me?* I wondered.

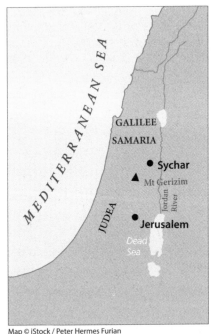

Map © iStock / Peter Hermes Furian

But as I neared, I recognized by His clothing that the man was a Jew, not one of my Samaritan neighbors. I breathed a sigh of relief. A Jewish man wouldn't speak to me; it was forbidden. I could fill my water jar and go back home.

However, the man didn't act like any Jew I had ever heard of. As I pulled up my jar of cool water, He said, "Give Me a drink." I shouldn't have been surprised, for the sun beat down and thirst is natural in this heat. But Jews avoided my people and *never* shared a drinking vessel.

When I mentioned this, the man said the most confusing thing: "If you knew God's gift and who is speaking to you now, you would ask for living water." This made no sense. The man had nothing to draw water with. How could He get living water?

He went on, "Everyone who drinks this water will get thirsty again. But the water I give will satisfy thirst forever."

Now I really paid attention. "Sir, please give me this water so I don't have to keep coming to this well!"

But then—instead of giving this amazing water—the man switched the subject. He said, "Go and get your husband."

I was ashamed to admit, "I don't have a husband."

Then the stranger totally astonished me. "That's true," He said. "You've had five husbands, but the man you have now isn't your husband."

How did He know that? I thought. *I've never met this man in my life.* "Sir," I said, "You must be a prophet." His prophetic skills intrigued me so I pursued an issue that had long troubled me. "My people worship on nearby Mount Gerizim, while Your people require worship in Jerusalem," I said.

The prophet didn't take sides on the proper place to worship. He instead told me that soon the place of worship wouldn't matter at all. He talked about worshiping in spirit and truth.

His words reminded me of what I had heard about a future Savior, so I said, "I know that when the Messiah comes, He will tell us everything."

The next words out of the stranger's mouth blew me away: "I am He."

Let me tell you, I was so stunned that I left my water jar behind and ran to get my neighbors. "Come," I said, "come see a man who told me all about everything I've done. Perhaps He's the Messiah!"

I doubted anyone from my town would listen to me. But they did.

And they listened to the stranger. Many of my neighbors also became convinced that this Jewish prophet was indeed the One we had been waiting for: the Promised One, who would save the world.

Now, days later, I returned to the well. As I balanced the water jar on my head with one hand and shielded my eyes from the morning sun with the other, I got in line at the well with my neighbors as we talked about all that had happened.

> **KEY VERSE**
>
> Many Samaritans from that town believed in Him because of the woman's testimony, "He told me all that I ever did." (John 4:39)

They say baseball is a game of failure. Players can fail seven out of ten times and still be considered a success. Still, a batter deals with failure every time they hear, "Strike!"

The Samaritan woman who met Jesus at the town well had multiple strikes against her. Her race, her gender, and her reputation all made her a washout in the ancient world. Yet although she was down in the count, Jesus did not declare her out. He welcomed her into the kingdom of God.

Setting the Scene

In the last chapter, we explored John the Baptist's well-known line "He must increase, but I must decrease." The prophet said this in response to the concern one of his followers had over the number of people going to Jesus and His disciples for Baptism.

In the next chapter of John, we discover that John's followers were not the only people who noticed Jesus' influence increasing. The apostle writes:

> Now when Jesus learned that the Pharisees had heard that Jesus was making and baptizing more disciples than John (although Jesus Himself did not baptize, but only His disciples), He left Judea and departed again for Galilee. And He had to pass through Samaria. (John 4:1–4)

Jesus didn't need to engage with the Pharisees at this early stage of His ministry, so He left Judea to journey north to Galilee. John 4:4 says that "He had to pass through Samaria." It is true that Samaria lay between Judea and Galilee with three different routes connecting the two lands. The most direct route went straight through Samaria. However, most Jews opted to either journey along the Mediterranean Sea or cross the Jordan and travel on the east side of the river until they were north of Samaria, where they would cross the river again and enter Galilee.[50]

Why would Jews avoid the direct route and choose an option that added a day or more to their trip? Because of the animosity between Jews and Samaritans.

The Jews wanted nothing to do with Samaritans because of their mixed heritage. Their history began in 722 BC when the Assyrians conquered the Northern Kingdom of Israel and destroyed the capital city of Samaria. Assyrian kings took many Israelite citizens to Assyria and imported people from other lands into Samaria. The Israelites left behind in Samaria intermarried with the immigrants. Since their descendants were no longer purely Jewish, people of pure Jewish descent looked down on the mixed-race Samaritans.

Another point of contention between the Jews and Samaritans existed in their worship practices. The Jews acknowledged all of Jewish scripture from Genesis to Malachi as God's Word, but the Samaritans accepted only the Five Books of Moses.[51] Because of this, the Samaritans rejected the temple in Jerusalem as the true place of worship. They instead worshiped at Mount Gerizim because Abraham had built an altar at Shechem, beneath Mount Gerizim. The place was important because the Israelites had entered Canaan and congregated at Mount Gerizim for a reading of God's Law and blessings (Deuteronomy 27:12; Joshua 8:33).[52]

The historian Josephus reported that in the fourth century BC, the Jewish high priest Manasseh married the daughter of a Samaritan named Sanballat. In response, the Jews threatened to expel Manasseh from Jerusalem. Sanballat built Manasseh a temple at Mount Gerizim similar to the one in Jerusalem to encourage Manasseh to stay with his daughter. This temple served as the center of Samaritan worship until 128 BC, when the Jewish king and priest John Hyrcanus conquered Samaria and destroyed the temple. Naturally, this heightened the hostility between the two peoples.[53] The hatred increased even more in AD 6–7 when some Samaritans attended Passover in Jerusalem and desecrated the temple by scattering bones in the sacred building.[54]

Given this history, we can better understand the animosity between Jews and Samaritans and see why the Jews preferred to take the long route to Galilee rather than deal with hated Samaritans.

MULTIPLE STRIKES

Scripture, however, tells us Jesus *"had* to pass through Samaria" (John 4:4, emphasis added). We know there were other routes, so why did He *have* to pass through Samaria? His compulsion was not geographical but theological. Jesus had a mission to meet a particular Samaritan woman. A woman who had multiple strikes against her.

THE WOMAN AT THE WELL

Scripture doesn't give the name of the woman at the well, but Eastern Christians have traditionally called her Photini, which means "light bearer." Jesus revealed Himself—the light of the world—to her. She, in turn, took that light to her neighbors.[55]

Strike 1: Race. As we have learned, Jews would have avoided her because of her race. As Jesus and His disciples walked through Samaria, there may have been some murmuring at the back of the pack: "Why go this way?" Regardless, they arrived at the village of Sychar at noon. Jesus sat at the neighborhood well to rest while His disciples went into town to buy food. The timing was perfect for meeting one Samaritan woman coming to the well for water.

THE SAMARITAN WOMAN HAD MULTIPLE STRIKES AGAINST HER.

Strike 2: Gender. Simply being a woman earned her another strike. In the culture of the day, men rarely spoke to women in public.[56] This was especially true for rabbis; a Jewish teacher would not even speak to his own wife in public.[57] The religious leaders considered women second-class citizens not worthy of theological education. Teaching a woman was considered a desecration of the sacred. "The rabbis said, 'It is better that the words of the law be burned than be delivered to a woman!'"[58] Yet Jesus waited at the well in order to speak with this particular female.

Strike 3: Reputation. But most shocking, Jesus singled out a woman with a sordid past. A woman with multiple marital failures. When Jesus told her to get her husband and come back, she replied, "I have no husband." To which Jesus said,

> You are right in saying, "I have no husband"; for you have had five husbands, and the one you now have is not your husband. What you have said is true. (John 4:17–18)

We don't know why the woman had so many husbands. Anyone hearing her story would probably assume her to be a woman of loose morals, but Scripture doesn't give us the details. Given the "no-fault" divorce practice of the day by which a husband could issue a certificate of divorce for any reason and turn his wife out into the street, we can imagine several scenarios. Did her husband reject her because of infertility? Was she then forced to find another husband because she had no means of support? Had one or more of her husbands died? Many possibilities exist, yet we can't ignore Jesus' statement about her current situation: "The one you now have is not your husband" (John 4:18). Her lifestyle at that moment was immoral.

Because of the time of day that she came to the well, many commentators speculate that she was a social outcast. Most women drew water in the cool of the morning rather than the heat of the day. John writes that Jesus met the woman at the well at the sixth hour (John 4:6). If John was using Jewish time, this would be noon; if Roman time, 6:00 a.m. But since she appears to be the only one at the well, it is logical to assume the noon time. Why would she haul water at noon rather than at a cooler time when she could also engage socially with other women of the town? Perhaps she chose to endure the sweltering heat rather than the icy-cold silence of her neighbors.

Jesus purposefully planned His itinerary to meet with this person who was considered racially inferior and of second-rate gender. He took a route that His people usually avoided to talk with a woman who had questionable morals and was shunned by society. Why choose her?

LEAST LIKELY TO SUCCEED

Have you ever met someone and thought, *That person will go places!* I remember thinking that about one of my fellow students in college. We were both music majors and sang in the same choir. But this woman also had talents in the theater and starred in many of the university's drama productions. While everyone on the stage of one of those shows did an admirable job, this woman outshone them all. The other actors knew their lines and delivered them well, but she *became* her character.

LIVING WATER

Back in chapter 4, where we studied Jeremiah, we learned about cisterns that stored rainwater. Yahweh complained that Israel had made broken cisterns for themselves and rejected God, "the fountain of living waters" (Jeremiah 2:13).

In John 4, Jesus uses the words "living water" while speaking to the Samaritan woman. This Hebrew phrase of "living water" indicated flowing water.[59] The well of Jacob at Sychar was a great improvement over a cistern that held stagnant rainwater, because it intercepted a fresh, flowing, underground stream.[60] But the "living water" Jesus spoke of surpasses any earthly water. The water Jesus gives quenches our deepest desire for relationship with God.

David wrote about this spiritual thirst: "My soul thirsts for God, for the living God" (Psalm 42:2). We may try many other things to satiate that thirst—money, relationships, success—but they will only satisfy temporarily. Jesus promised to fill our souls permanently: "Whoever drinks of the water that I will give him will never be thirsty again. The water that I will give him will become in him a spring of water welling up to eternal life" (John 4:14). Jesus gives us the gift of living water that will daily give us strength but also grant eternal life.

After graduation, I heard she went to the famed Yale School of Drama. A few years later, our university alumni paper highlighted her career on Broadway. "I knew she would make it!" I said when I read the article. Since then, I've seen her in movies and television shows. My fellow classmate whom I thought "most likely to succeed" actually did!

I doubt the villagers of Sychar would have given this woman the label "Most Likely to Succeed." Just the opposite. After all, she couldn't seem to keep a husband. She lived with a man who didn't even give her the dignity of legal marriage.

Isn't it just like Jesus to choose "the least likely to succeed"? He could have chosen to meet with kings or governors, high priests or scribes. Yet He chose a woman who had experienced prejudice and rejection. Someone who perhaps didn't have a single friend. Her solitary visit to the community well was the perfect time to tell her the Good News about living water.

Jesus started the conversation by simply asking for a drink. His request shocked her because Jews normally avoided all contact with her race. Jesus continued by telling her about living water, and she became confused. How could this stranger get this living water? He didn't even have anything to draw water with.

Jesus explained,

> Everyone who drinks of this water will be thirsty again, but whoever drinks of the water that I will give him will never be thirsty again. The water that I will give him will become in him a spring of water welling up to eternal life. (John 4:13–14)

The woman saw the advantage of this water—no more backbreaking work of hauling water in the heat of the day. She said, "Sir, give me this water" (v. 15).

Then Jesus turned the conversation in a different direction. "Go, call your husband, and come here" (John 4:16). Jesus had told her the truth of the Gospel, but now He spoke words of Law: "Only this way could she realize the thirst that Jesus quenches forever. When He told her to get her husband, He effectively showed her sin to her and gave her the opportunity to confess."[61]

She admitted, "I have no husband" (v. 17), and this one sentence gave Jesus an opportunity to demonstrate His omniscience: "You are right in saying, 'I have no husband'; for you have had five husbands, and the one you now have is not your husband. What you have said is true" (vv. 17–18).

His knowledge about her made her wonder if this Jew could be the One her people had waited for. She told Jesus, "I know that Messiah is coming

(He who is called Christ). When He comes, He will tell us all things" (v. 25).

Then Jesus did something even more surprising—He revealed His identity: "I who speak to you am He" (v. 26). This is the first time in Scripture that Jesus clearly identified Himself as the Messiah, and He didn't do it again until His trial, when the high priest asked, "Are You the Christ, the Son of the Blessed?" (Mark 14:61). There, Jesus responded, "I am" (v. 62), and the religious leaders immediately condemned Him to death. But revealing Himself in Samaria did not have the same dangers, because Samaritans didn't think of the Messiah as a political figure but as a teacher who would reveal God's will.[62]

Still, I find it surprising that Jesus would make this declaration of His divinity and purpose to an outcast, a lowly woman with a problematic lifestyle. He revealed Himself to someone most would consider the least likely to succeed.

Yet she did succeed. When she encountered someone who knew all about her past but spoke without the disgust she saw in other people's eyes, she knew she needed to tell her neighbors. Although she probably steered clear of the townspeople most of the time, now she sought them out! Though she likely avoided mentioning her past, meeting Jesus made her tell everyone in Sychar, "Come, see a man who told me all that I ever did. Can this be the Christ?" (John 4:29).

Perhaps the townspeople were so shocked that this woman spoke to them that they had to see who could cause such a stunning change. Many people did go to the well to see Jesus (v. 30). And their encounter with Him did not simply mean satisfying their curiosity, for "many Samaritans from that town believed in Him because of the woman's testimony" (v. 39). God used this least-likely-to-succeed woman to tell a whole town about Him.

Do you sometimes see yourself as the least likely to succeed? Maybe you didn't go to college or finish high school. Or you believe you're too shy or too loud or not well-spoken enough to be an effective witness. You think you're not talented enough, smart enough, or popular enough to make a difference. But the Samaritan woman's story reassures us that achievement in God's kingdom doesn't hinge on our own abilities or popularity. Jesus can use those "least likely to succeed" to bring many people to faith.

JESUS CAN USE THOSE "LEAST LIKELY TO SUCCEED" TO BRING MANY PEOPLE TO FAITH.

FINDING LIVING WATER IN ILLINOIS

The story of the Samaritan woman and her compulsion to tell the Good News of the Messiah reminds me of a woman I know who shares the urgency to tell others about Christ. Years ago, Mariaisabel Morales moved to my town of Aurora, Illinois, from her hometown of Mexico City, Mexico. Her husband, Angel, had a vision of a better life for them in this country. Mariaisabel had no desire to leave her family and homeland, but she and their two-year-old son came so they could all be together. Yet, although their little family all lived in the same place, they still weren't truly together. The parents each worked two jobs just to get by. Mariaisabel didn't see how this was a better life.

When their second child arrived, they were happy, but the situation did not improve. They tried to fit into the culture, but the culture only encouraged them to work hard, earn money, and buy things. Angel and Mariaisabel's marriage began to suffer.

As problems increased, Mariaisabel convinced Angel that she needed to stay home with the children, and she encouraged Angel to spend one day each week with the family. When he agreed to no work on Sundays, Mariaisabel made a list of activities to do together.

Number one on the list? Go to church.

Mariaisabel might not have included this activity except for a conversation with her father. He had asked her, "Where is God in your life?" She had answered, "I ask God for help with my husband. Help for my kids. But He doesn't seem to answer." Her father pressed, "But where is God in *your* life?" She realized she had not made space for God.

Like the woman at the well, Mariaisabel was thirsty, and her thirst for God led them to Iglesia Evangelica Luterana San Pablo (St. Paul Lutheran Church). She enjoyed the services, but at first Angel was skeptical. He asked the pastor many questions, took notes, and then searched through the Bible when they returned home. At first, Angel wanted to prove the pastor wrong so he had a reason to quit attending the weekly services. But the more time he spent in Scripture, the more God changed his heart.

In fact, Angel also developed a spiritual thirst that eventually led him to the seminary. Initially, this made life more difficult financially. Mariaisabel rejoiced that her husband now sought the living water of Jesus, but this meant Angel didn't have as much time to work to support the family. Unpaid bills sometimes meant no gas, no electricity, no water. They even lost their house. But this loss didn't worry Mariaisabel, because that became the point when she finally felt at home in their new country.

Now when Mariaisabel looks back on their journey, she sees that every single moment, they were in the hands of the Father. He had a plan for them all along. They both currently serve at St. Paul Lutheran Church. Angel works as the pastor of Spanish Ministry and Mariaisabel serves as a deaconess—a professional church worker trained to share the Gospel of Jesus through teaching, caring for others spiritually, and works of mercy.[63]

"ONCE YOU KNOW JESUS, IT'S IMPOSSIBLE TO BE THE SAME PERSON."

Mariaisabel wanted professional training to help people in her community. She sees other people on the same path she and her husband took. They come to this country thirsting for new life, and she wants to make sure they know that Jesus is the source of living water and new life, the only one who can satisfy souls. Like the woman at the well, she can't keep quiet about the Messiah.

Mariaisabel says, "Once you know Jesus, it's impossible to be the same person. You have to tell everyone. He is everything you need. You will have problems, but the problems don't consume you, because He is with you. He has a plan for you."

WORSHIP

When Jesus exposed the woman's multiple relationship failures, she changed the subject: "Sir, I perceive that You are a prophet. Our fathers worshiped on this mountain, but You say that in Jerusalem is the place where people ought to worship" (John 4:19–20). Many commentators suppose that she turned the conversation in another direction because she didn't want to talk about her own failures. But Gary P. Baumler in his commentary on John has another take:

> Just as likely, however, now that her sin was out and acknowledged, she was concerned with her spiritual welfare and turned her attention to matters of worship. Where could she go to confess to God and be cleansed of her sin?[64]

Perhaps she brought up the topic of worship because she realized her desperate need for God. Jesus' answer to her may support this theory, as He avoids talking about the controversy of the place of worship and instead tells her, "True worshipers will worship the Father in spirit and truth" (John 4:23). He wants the Samaritan woman to know that true worship does not depend on place or particular forms. True worship depends on the Holy Spirit's leading.

WHEN YOU FEEL YOU HAVE STRUCK OUT

What do we do when life feels like a string of failures? We see from the life of the woman at the well that even when we have multiple strikes against us, God doesn't shout, "You're out!" Her story teaches us about success in God's kingdom.

Success does not depend on our gender, race, or reputation. The woman at the well had nothing to qualify her for success in her culture. As a female, she was considered a second-class citizen, one not worthy to learn about things of God. Her Samaritan race was considered inferior because of its mixed ancestry. And her reputation? Well, let's just say her neighbors probably didn't invite her to the neighborhood barbecues.

Yet Jesus timed His journey to Galilee to meet with the woman, to teach her about living water, and to tell her about worshiping in spirit and truth. He chose to reveal His true identity to someone most people overlooked. He picked *her* to tell other Samaritans about the Savior of the world. "Come and see," she told the people of Sychar. We don't need a degree in theology to share our faith. We can simply tell others about the difference the Messiah makes in our lives.

You might think your gender or race limits the influence you have. Or that your lack of a big platform means your reach will be small. You might believe your reputation or past will prevent others from listening to you. If so, remember that Jesus used a woman with all of these strikes against her to bring many people to faith. Jesus can use you, too, right where you are. Think of Mariaisabel, who came to this country without knowing the language and yet completed formal training in theology so she could better tell others about Christ. Let's all tell the people around us, "Come and see."

We don't need to hide our past in order to achieve success. It's believed that the Samaritan woman came to the well at noon to avoid her neighbors who may have shunned her because of her past. Rather than endure the shaming, she avoided it. Then Jesus used her past to draw her to Him. His knowledge about everything she ever did proved to her that He was the Messiah. She was astounded at what He knew but maybe even more surprised at His lack of disdain. He knew everything about her, yet He still spoke to her with respect and compassion.

Jesus knows all about your past too. He knows all about the lie you told to get the job and the gossip you carelessly spread. He knows about the big mistake you made in the backseat of your boyfriend's car years ago and the harsh words you hurled at your spouse yesterday.

Yet Jesus purposely seeks you out. As He did with the Samaritan woman, He will confront you with your sin, but He does so with an offer of

THE SAMARITAN WOMAN: FIVE-TIME FAILURE

grace to cover it all. He loves you no matter what you've done. Jesus wants you to know that nothing in your past prohibits you from receiving His living water.

JESUS WANTS YOU TO KNOW THAT NOTHING IN YOUR PAST PROHIBITS YOU FROM RECEIVING HIS LIVING WATER.

In reality, our past stories may be exactly what draws people to Jesus. Although the woman probably avoided talking about her past, when she dropped her water jar to tell her neighbors about the Messiah, she said, "Come, see a man who told me all that I ever did" (John 4:29). Her broken past no longer made her hide. Her neighbors saw the dramatic change in her, and they were pulled to the Savior.

EVANGELISM

Lessons on evangelism often use the story of the woman at the well. After all, the account has two inspiring models to follow.

First, notice how Jesus approached the Samaritan woman. He started a conversation by talking about an everyday activity. He used her current actions to start a spiritual conversation. He didn't begin by confronting her with her sin, but by making her aware of her spiritual thirst. He then drew attention to her shortcomings and her need for a Savior.

The Samaritan woman also offers an excellent model of evangelism. She didn't wait until she had memorized a four-point outline of a plan of salvation or completed a nine-week training course in telling about Jesus. She simply went to her neighbors and told them about her encounter with the Savior.

I ask myself, "How can I use everyday conversations to steer the topic to spiritual needs? How can I share the miraculous ways that Jesus has changed my life?"

When I began speaking to women's groups, I met another speaker from the same organization. This woman had a dynamic story. Before she knew Jesus, she worked as a bartender and sold cocaine on the side. She never used drugs herself but made a tidy profit dealing them. Although she might have felt uncomfortable talking about her outrageous past, she didn't hesitate to do so because in telling her backstory, others could see the change Christ had worked in her heart and life.

Have you tried to hide your past failures and mistakes? Perhaps you, like the woman at the well, can use them to draw people to Jesus.

Multiple failures do not disqualify us from success in God's kingdom. The Samaritan woman had numerous failures, including the loss of five husbands. "The Jews held that a woman might be divorced twice or at the most three times. If the Samaritans had the same standard, this woman's life had been exceedingly immoral."[65] Of course, we don't know her backstory, but probably everyone in her community would have viewed her as a repeat offender. Did the woman see herself the same way? Men discarded her. Women turned away. Maybe she thought she had messed up too many times for God to forgive her.

Sometimes our culture views God as a sort of cosmic scale. *If my good deeds outweigh the bad*, people think, *then I'll go to heaven.* Of course, this isn't true. One tiny sin tips the scale to our eternal punishment as much as ten thousand sins. Only God's grace can tip the scale in our favor. Jesus' death and resurrection outweigh all of our sins and enable us to live with Him forever.

God's Measure of Success

Although most of us believe the truth of God's grace, we might not live it. We may think, *If my church knew how many times I snapped at my kids this week, they wouldn't let me in.* Or, *If my Bible study friends knew how many men I was with in college, they would ask me to leave.* While it's true we humans often act in harsh judgment of others, we see in the Samaritan woman's story that Jesus doesn't see multiple failures as a deal breaker.

When we trust in His saving work on the cross, He wipes out millions of sins as easily as He erases one. And when He has wiped them away, He sees us as clean as new-fallen snow. He used the woman with five failed marriages to change a whole town. However many times you've messed up, He still calls you to have faith in Him and still uses you to influence your world.

THE LORD USES PEOPLE WITH MULTIPLE FAILURES FOR STAGGERING SUCCESS IN HIS KINGDOM.

In our culture, the wealthy, the privileged, and the supertalented succeed. Those who experience even a little success are more likely to get noticed. Once they've made it to the first rung of the ladder of achievement, they have a better chance of climbing to the top.

But in God's kingdom, we see over and over again how Jesus picks the least likely. He welcomes those the world has shunned. He chooses to reveal Himself to people society ignores or has rejected. God's love doesn't depend on our perfection, for we are measured by grace. The Lord uses people with multiple failures for staggering success in His kingdom.

CHAPTER 7

MAY 10/

PETER: DYNAMIC DENIER

TIMELINE

Joseph	1915 BC
Rahab	1406 BC
David	1010 BC
Jeremiah	628 BC
John the Baptist	1st Century AD
Samaritan Woman	1st Century AD
Peter	1st Century AD

Peter focused on putting one foot in front of the other as he walked toward Jerusalem. It was all he could muster, given the weight lodged in his heart and the questions swirling in his mind. He barely registered the bright morning sunshine or the birds singing in the trees. They felt incongruous with what had happened in the past few days.

A few hours earlier, the women had burst into the room to tell him and the other disciples that the stone had been rolled away from the tomb. They described the angel who said,

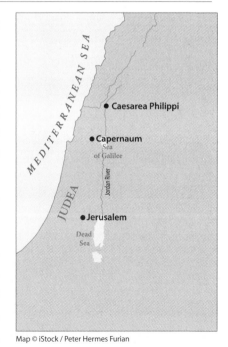

Map © iStock / Peter Hermes Furian

"Jesus isn't here! He is risen from the dead!" Most of the disciples had declared the news nonsense, but Peter and John had to see for themselves. Their feet flew along the road. John beat Peter to the tomb, but when he paused at the entrance, Peter rushed past and saw all the linen cloths used to wrap Jesus' body simply lying there—empty. The cloth that had covered Jesus' head lay neatly folded, separate from the other strips of linen.

Peter now trudged along the road, unable to comprehend what he had seen in the tomb. Could Jesus actually be alive? It seemed too good to believe. If he let his mind go there, disappointment would crush him if he found out that someone had maliciously stolen his friend's body.

Yet, why would grave robbers remove the linen strips? Why would they take the time to neatly fold the face cloth? And although some of the other men discounted the women's story of an angel, Peter wondered, *Why would they make up a tale like that?*

While Peter's mind spun with these questions, another, more terrible thought intruded: *Even if Jesus has risen, would He even talk to me?* Only a few days ago, Peter had denied knowing the man with whom he had spent the last three years. He cringed at the memory. He recalled his bold declaration to Jesus, "I'm ready to die with You," and Jesus' warning, "Before the rooster crows, you will deny even knowing Me." Peter had almost laughed at that—he had complete confidence in his dedication to Jesus.

Then everything had gone wrong. A crowd of men with swords and clubs came to arrest Jesus. Peter tried to stop them and even slashed at the ear of the high priest's slave. Someone had to stop this madness!

Yet Jesus calmly healed the man's ear and said something confusing about angels and fulfilling the Scriptures. Jesus *allowed* the guards to tie His hands and lead Him away.

Peter had followed at what he hoped was a safe distance to the home of the high priest, where Jesus had been taken. In the courtyard, guards stood near the fire, holding out their palms to the warmth. Weary servants tried to stay awake. It didn't take long for the accusations to start flying.

His heart sank as he recalled his words, "I don't know the man!" It seemed to Peter that all of his confidence and courage had stayed in the Garden of Gethsemane, for he found himself denying Jesus again and again.

That was three days ago. Now Peter stopped walking and put his head in his hands as he recalled the sound of the rooster's crow and the sight of Jesus' direct gaze. *What have I done?* Even if Jesus were alive, He wouldn't want anything to do with a man who denied knowing his best friend. Peter lowered his hands and started walking again. He needed the comfort of the other disciples, even if he didn't deserve to be with them anymore.

Just then, Peter saw someone walking toward him. Were his eyes deceiving him? It looked like Jesus. And He was smiling.

KEY VERSE

Simon, Simon, behold, Satan demanded to have you, that he might sift you like wheat, but I have prayed for you that your faith may not fail. And when you have turned again, strengthen your brothers. (Luke 22:31–32)

Success in the business world often means climbing the corporate ladder. Men and women vie for higher and higher company positions, hoping for the impressive titles and grand offices that come with them. This kind of success is a game of comparison: *Where do I stand? Who is above me? Who is below?*

During his time with Jesus, Peter tended to play the game of comparison and debated with other disciples about who was the greatest among them. Jesus taught humility, but even His closest followers didn't grasp that God's kingdom did not have the same hierarchy as the kingdom of the world.

SETTING THE SCENE

For years, I thought that the first time Jesus met Peter, Andrew, James, and John was when He called them to leave their fishing boats and follow

Him. But closer examination showed me that they had actually met Jesus some time before.

The story of Peter, the impetuous disciple, begins with a story of John the Baptist. One day when John stood talking with two of his disciples, Jesus walked by and John declared, "Behold, the Lamb of God!" (John 1:36). The two disciples of John the Baptist immediately followed Jesus and spent the day with Him. One of the men, Andrew, became so certain of Jesus' true identity that he went to his brother, Peter, and told him, "We have found the Messiah" (v. 41) and brought him to Jesus.

Jesus looked at Peter and said, "'You are Simon the son of John. You shall be called Cephas' (which means Peter)" (v. 42). So began Peter's journey with Jesus. Some time passed. Peter might have gone with Jesus to the wedding at Cana (John 2) and heard Him teach in Galilean synagogues (Luke 4:14–30). Perhaps as much as a year went by before Jesus called the fisherman to become a fisher of men:

> On one occasion, while the crowd was pressing in on Him to hear the word of God, He was standing by the lake of Gennesaret, and He saw two boats by the lake, but the fishermen had gone out of them and were washing their nets. Getting into one of the boats, which was Simon's, He asked him to put out a little from the land. And He sat down and taught the people from the boat. And when He had finished speaking, He said to Simon, "Put out into the deep and let down your nets for a catch." And Simon answered, "Master, we toiled all night and took nothing! But at Your word I will let down the nets." And when they had done this, they enclosed a large number of fish, and their nets were breaking. They signaled to their partners in the other boat to come and help them. And they came and filled both the boats, so that they began to sink. But when Simon Peter saw it, he fell down at Jesus' knees, saying, "Depart from me, for I am a sinful man, O Lord." For he and all who were with him were astonished at the catch of fish that they had taken, and so also were James and John, sons of

Zebedee, who were partners with Simon. And Jesus said to Simon, "Do not be afraid; from now on you will be catching men." And when they had brought their boats to land, they left everything and followed Him. (Luke 5:1–11)

Since Peter had known Jesus for months and had heard Him preach, it doesn't seem out of place for him to allow the man from Nazareth to use his boat as a pulpit. But I'm a little surprised that the professional fisherman took fishing advice from a carpenter. And I'm astonished that four men left their boats and livelihood to follow an itinerant preacher.

Even so, Peter's response to the miracle of the fish helps us understand. He had already spent time with Jesus. He had heard Him preach. He had probably seen Jesus heal people. Then this miracle of providing fish when they had found none all night demonstrated Jesus' power over creation.

SIMON PETER

When Jesus first met Simon, He changed the future disciple's name to Peter (John 1:42). In Jesus' day, *Simon* was the most common name in the land. However the Greek name *Peter* didn't come into use until the second or third century. And *Cephas*, the word in Aramaic, wasn't even used as a personal name.[66] We might wonder why Jesus would give Simon a name meaning "rock," because Peter didn't always display a rocklike faithfulness.

Although Jesus assigned the name Peter to this outspoken disciple, He usually used the name Simon. Later in His ministry, when Simon declared Jesus to be the Christ, Jesus said, "And I tell you, you are Peter, and on this rock I will build My church, and the gates of hell shall not prevail against it" (Matthew 16:18). Most scholars agree that the "rock" was Peter's confession of faith, not Peter himself. Over Peter's lifetime, Jesus transformed an ordinary man with a common name into a pillar of the Early Church.

Peter saw Jesus for who He was and fell in the sand at Jesus' knees. He cried out, "Depart from me!" because he clearly saw his own sinful condition. He knew sin could not stand in the presence of divinity. Peter's realization of Jesus' holiness led him, in a moment of astounding professional success, to give up everything to follow Him.

Progressive Failure

Peter's life with Jesus wasn't a long string of successes. The bold, impulsive disciple got himself into trouble, but his failures often began with stupendous success. For instance, when Jesus walked on water to meet His disciples in the middle of the Sea of Galilee, Peter was the only one with faith enough to say, "Lord, if it is You, command me to come to You on the water" (Matthew 14:28). He alone stepped out of the boat onto the water. Then he sank like a rock when he failed to keep his eyes on Jesus.

A little later on, Jesus took His disciples to Caesarea Philippi and asked them, "Who do people say that the Son of Man is?" (Matthew 16:13). They replied, "Some say John the Baptist, others say Elijah, and others Jeremiah or one of the prophets" (v. 14). Then Jesus made it more personal: "But who do you say that I am?" (v. 15). And Peter, as spokesman for the group, made a bold confession of faith: "You are the Christ, the Son of the living God" (v. 16). Jesus commended Peter, telling him the Father had revealed this truth to him. But when Jesus went on to teach His disciples that He would need to suffer, die, and rise again, Peter rebuked Jesus (something unthinkable for a disciple to do to his master).[67] He said, "Far be it from You, Lord! This shall never happen to You" (v. 22). At this, Jesus turned to Peter and said, "Get behind Me, Satan! You are a hindrance to Me. For you are not setting your mind on the things of God, but on the things of man" (v. 23). Peter succeeded in identifying Jesus as the Messiah, but he failed to understand what being the Messiah meant.

In the Garden of Gethsemane, Peter again began with confidence but experienced another failure of comprehension. On the way to His favorite prayer spot, Jesus had warned the disciples that all of them would desert Him. He specifically told Peter, "Truly, I tell you, this very night, before the rooster crows, you will deny Me three times" (Matthew 26:34). Plucky Peter couldn't imagine this scenario. He boasted, "Even if I must die with You, I will not deny You!" (v. 35).

After that bit of bravado, Peter was probably as surprised as anyone at the events that happened only a few hours later. When Judas came with a crowd of men with clubs and swords, Peter must have watched in confusion as Jesus allowed them to tie His hands and lead Him away. Until that point, Peter probably expected Jesus to be the type of Christ that would free the Jews from Roman oppression. A powerful deliverer. A victorious conqueror. *Not* someone who would submit to the current powers in Jerusalem. The ear-slashing disciple failed to grasp Jesus' true mission.

Peter used his last bit of courage to follow Jesus at a distance as the guards led Him to the home of the high priest. Perhaps everything would have been fine if one sassy servant girl hadn't stared at Peter and said, "You also were with Jesus the Galilean" (v. 69). Peter tried to evade her accusation by saying, "I do not know what you mean" (v. 70).

Peter then stepped away from the fire and stood at the entrance of the courtyard. Did his conscience bother him? Did he feel he was in danger, staying so close to Jesus? Did he hope to avoid any more questions? But stepping away didn't stop the accusations. Another servant girl saw Peter in the doorway and announced to everyone nearby, "This man was with Jesus of Nazareth" (v. 71). Peter's denial then escalated. He replied with an oath: "I do not know the man" (v. 72). This wasn't a case of potty mouth but a call on something sacred to give assurance that he spoke truthfully.[68]

An hour passed. What went through Peter's mind during those sixty minutes? Perhaps he wanted to run away, yet couldn't bear to leave Jesus. Maybe he already felt the sing of conscience. But another person came up to Peter and said, "Certainly you too are one of them, for your accent betrays you" (v. 73). Judeans thought Galileans like Peter didn't properly pronounce guttural sounds and considered them backward.[69] Once more, Peter failed to measure up. "He began to invoke a curse on himself and to swear, 'I do not know the man'" (v. 74).

Before Peter even stopped speaking, a rooster crowed. From across the courtyard, Jesus turned and looked at him (Luke 22:60–61). Can you imagine what Peter felt when he met Jesus' eyes? Luke uses the Greek word *emblepo* when describing Jesus' gaze. *Emblepo* "describes a person looking specifically at someone or something. The prefix *em-* usually adds a note of intensity."[70] Mark also uses this word to describe the way the first servant girl looked at Peter when she accused him of being with Jesus. We might say she glared at him. But Mark also uses *emblepo* in the story of the rich young ruler who was unwilling to give up his wealth to follow Jesus: "And Jesus, looking at [*emblepo*] him, loved him" (Mark 10:21). This is the look I think Jesus gave Peter. Intense? Sad and disappointed? Yes. Angry and accusing? I don't think so. I think Jesus looked at Peter earnestly and loved him.

ALTHOUGH JESUS SAW PETER AT HIS WORST AND SEES US WHEN WE FAIL, HE WENT TO THE CROSS TO TAKE THE PUNISHMENT WE ALL DESERVED.

Again we see how God included stories of human failure in His Word to comfort us. We can all relate to Peter because at times we have all hidden our association with Jesus just to fit in. We knew what we were doing was wrong, but we did it anyway. Nevertheless, we still have God's grace. "Self-preservation is never justification for denying our Lord and His tie with us. Jesus ever looks at us in love to call us to repentance, forgiving our sins."[71] Although Jesus saw Peter at his worst and sees us when we fail, He went to the cross to take the punishment we all deserved.

PROGRESSIVE SUCCESS

I can imagine that Jesus' look, even if loving, slashed at Peter's heart just as he had slashed the servant's ear. That look probably cut out any self-confidence still lingering in Peter's soul. He had completely failed Jesus. Perhaps he wondered, *How can I have any place in God's kingdom after what I have done?*

But Jesus didn't leave Peter stuck in his failure or wondering about his position in the Kingdom. We see God's grace to Peter in John 21 in an incident after Jesus' resurrection.

Much like the fishing story that happened the day Jesus called Peter, Andrew, James, and John, several of the disciples went out in the boat but caught nothing. At dawn, someone onshore called out to them, "Children, do you have any fish?" (John 21:5). The disciples told the man no, and He instructed them to throw the net on the other side of the boat. When they did, the net was so full of fish that they couldn't haul it into the boat. That's when they recognized that the man was Jesus.

The disciples rowed back to shore, dragging the overflowing net behind them. When they reached land, they saw Jesus had prepared a fish breakfast for them over a charcoal fire.

When Peter finished breakfast, Jesus pulled him aside for a private conversation. Three times Jesus asked, "Simon, son of John, do you love Me?" and three times Peter replied, "Yes, Lord; You know that I love You" (vv. 15–17). Jesus gave Peter three opportunities to declare his love, countering Peter's three denials. In Peter's answers, we see a totally different character. No more bravado like before when he proclaimed he would never abandon the Lord. Instead, Peter put the focus on Jesus and humbly appealed to his Savior's ability to see into his heart: "Lord, You know everything; You know that I love You" (v. 17).[72]

In this exchange, Peter discovered that his failure didn't disqualify him from service. He had no need to fear for his place in the Kingdom. After each of Peter's confessions of love, Jesus gave Peter a duty: "Feed My lambs. . . . Tend My sheep. . . . Feed My sheep." The Lord charged Peter with giving spiritual nourishment to the Shepherd's flock through Word and Sacrament. He appointed Peter to give guidance and comfort to Jesus' lambs and sheep.[73]

One thing I love about this story is that Jesus didn't ask Peter, "Will you promise to never again mess up or let Me down?" He asked only, "Do

JESUS DIDN'T ASK PETER, "WILL YOU PROMISE TO NEVER AGAIN MESS UP?" HE ASKED ONLY, "DO YOU LOVE ME?" you love Me?" This tells me that achievement in God's kingdom doesn't mean doing everything perfectly. It means loving God with heart, soul, and mind and reveling in friendship with Him. Jesus doesn't glare at us and demand, "Promise you will never fail again!" No, He looks at each of us with compassion and asks, "Do you love Me?"

Peter did go on to demonstrate his love for Jesus by feeding and tending the Shepherd's lambs. On Pentecost, he gave a powerful sermon. No longer running on the low-octane fuel of his own bravado but now filled with the high-octane power of the Holy Spirit, Peter led three thousand people to faith in Christ that day.

Peter's story fills the first twelve chapters of the Book of Acts. He performed a miraculous healing of a lame beggar in chapter 3. He presided over the strange case of lying Ananias and Sapphira in chapter 5. Through the power of God, he brought Tabitha back to life in chapter 9. With the help of an angel, he escaped from prison in chapter 12.

After Acts 15, the Bible doesn't tell us any more about Peter's life. But other sources explain that both Peter and Paul were in Rome in July of AD 64—a time marked by Nero's persecution of the Church. Eusebius, a historian of Christianity, wrote that Paul, as a Roman citizen, was beheaded. But Peter "was crucified upside down in the Circus of Nero, 'near the obelisk between the goals,' where the Vatican now stands."[74] In the end, Peter did die defending the Lord he loved.

WHEN YOU FALL FLAT

Don't you love Peter? So many times he boldly strove for success, only to fall flat. We can all relate to his fumbling attempts to follow Jesus. Let's learn from his failures and successes.

Failure is an opportunity to realize our need for God's grace. Before the night of Jesus' arrest, Peter had no doubt in his ability to remain faithful to the Teacher. Can't you see his chest puff out as he confidently declares,

"I will not deny You" (Matthew 26:35)? Perhaps his abundant self-reliance led him to sleep in the garden instead of praying to avoid temptation as Jesus had advised. Perhaps Peter didn't even see his need for grace. Just a few hours later, Peter broke his promises of loyalty. Leaning on his own courage proved disastrous.

I can so relate. My sinful nature tells me to believe in my own strength. And when I trust in my own capacity to accomplish things, I may ignore my need for grace. But when I've fallen flat on my face, crushed by the evidence of my pride, I have no doubt about the necessity of God's grace. At such times, a little detail in Peter's story gives me comfort.

In Luke's account of Jesus predicting Peter's denial, he records Jesus' words to His bumbling disciple: "Simon, Simon, behold, Satan demanded to have you, that he might sift you like wheat, but I have prayed for you that your faith may not fail. And when you have turned again, strengthen your brothers" (Luke 22:31–32). In the Greek, the first sentence uses the plural form of the word *you*. Jesus told His disciples, "Satan wants to sift *all of you* like wheat." The devil hoped that when he shook Jesus' followers, he would find only worthless chaff. But in the second sentence, *you* is singular. Jesus specifically prayed for Peter because He knew Peter would deny Him and that the failure would crush Peter's spirit. Jesus prayed that Peter's faith would not fail completely.[75]

Just as Jesus saw Peter heading for failure, He looks ahead on my personal timeline and sees when I will be tempted to work for my glory instead of His or keep quiet about my faith for fear of what others will think. And just as Jesus prayed for Peter, He intercedes for me. Romans 8:34 says, "Christ Jesus is the one who died—more than that, who was raised—who is at the right hand of God, who indeed is interceding for us." My Savior intercedes to the Father and gives me the humility to work for His honor and the strength to share my faith.

JESUS KNOWS I CAN'T AVOID FAILURE BY MYSELF, SO *HE* INTERCEDES FOR ME.

WATCH AND PRAY

Jesus graciously prayed for Peter, but He also instructed Peter to pray. After Peter, James, and John fell asleep in the Garden of Gethsemane, Jesus said, "Simon, are you asleep? Could you not watch one hour? Watch and pray that you may not enter into temptation. The spirit indeed is willing, but the flesh is weak" (Mark 14:37–38).

Jesus taught all of His disciples to take temptation seriously when He included this petition in the Lord's Prayer: "And lead us not into temptation" (Matthew 6:13). Martin Luther wrote this in his explanation of this petition:

> God tempts no one. We pray in this petition that God would guard and keep us so that the devil, the world, and our sinful nature may not deceive us or mislead us into false belief, despair, and other great shame and vice. Although we are attacked by these things, we pray that we may finally overcome them and win the victory.[76]

I hate to admit it, but my prayers usually revolve around my needs and my wants. But Jesus wants me to recognize that temptation lies right around the corner. If I want to resist it, then I need to pray accordingly, relying on God's strength instead of my own.

God does not define success as being better than someone else. Throughout Jesus' time with His closest followers, we see these twelve men argue about which of them is the greatest. One such debate took place shortly after Jesus' transfiguration and immediately after He told them about His impending death. How could the disciples even think about their personal rank after seeing Jesus in His shining glory? How could they quarrel over their own status when their best friend had told them He would soon die?

A similar argument took place at the Last Supper. Right after Jesus told the disciples that one of them would betray Him, "a dispute also arose among them, as to which of them was to be regarded as the greatest" (Luke 22:24). Really, guys? Your esteemed teacher has just told you a member of your group is about to turn on Him, and you argue about who has reached a higher rung of importance?

Even after Jesus' resurrection, we find Peter comparing himself with others. At the end of the account of Jesus questioning Peter about his love for Him, Jesus gave Peter a hint about how he would die: "Truly, truly, I say to you, when you were young, you used to dress yourself and walk wherever you wanted, but when you are old, you will stretch out your hands, and another will dress you and carry you where you do not want to go" (John 21:18).[77] Peter didn't seem to have any questions about his own death, but when he saw John nearby, he asked, "Lord, what about this man?" (v. 21). Jesus replied, "If it is My will that he remain until I come, what is that to you? You follow Me!" (v. 22). In other words, "Don't concern yourself about the faith walk of someone else. Concentrate on following Me."

I don't know about you, but I tend to follow Peter's practice of comparison and measure myself against others. I compare myself to the speaker who got the higher billing and to best-selling authors. I feel like I don't measure up. Social media makes evaluating ourselves against others easy by quantifying our popularity in likes and shares. Even in Christian circles, we might judge value by the church that has more people in the pews or kids at VBS. But Jesus reminds us, "What is that to you? Focus on your walk with Me. Your place in God's kingdom isn't measured by who's more important. If anything, greatness in My kingdom comes through aiming to be *lower* on the ladder, not *higher*." (See Luke 22:26.)

When we have failed, we can still run to Jesus. Notice I didn't write *if* we have failed but *when*. Because of our humanness, we will trip up in following God's commands. We will say the wrong thing or neglect to do the right thing. Maybe our collapse won't match the magnitude of Judas's or Peter's, but we will experience significant failure. And when that happens, we

JESUS TELLS US, "DON'T COMPARE YOURSELF TO OTHERS. CONCENTRATE ON FOLLOWING ME."

need to realize we have a choice. We can wallow in guilt like Judas. Or we can receive forgiveness like Peter.

Before embarking on this in-depth study of Peter, I had glossed over an important detail in the Gospel of Luke. When the two men on the road to Emmaus returned to Jerusalem to tell the disciples about seeing the resurrected Savior, Jesus' disciples told the men from Emmaus, "The Lord has risen indeed, and has appeared to Simon!" (Luke 24:34). That tells us Jesus met Peter privately before He appeared to the whole group.

In the opening of this chapter, I pictured Peter meeting Jesus on his way back from the tomb. Scripture gives us no details of the meeting, yet we can imagine what that meeting might have been like: Peter a mess of joy at seeing Jesus and grief at knowing he had betrayed Him. Jesus holding out His nail-scarred hands to Peter, letting him know his failure did not mean an end to their relationship. I find it so touching that Jesus took time for a personal and private meeting to reassure the repentant disciple of His love.

JESUS HAS ALREADY WASHED AWAY YOUR SIN AND SHAME.

We all need this reassurance when we think our failures are too big for forgiveness and we begin to sink in shame. A woman I know constantly struggles with guilt even though all her friends would describe her as a wonderful person. Intellectually, she knows Jesus' death has paid for all her wrongs, yet she can't seem to accept that reality in a way that frees her from the burden of self-reproach. When I told her about Jesus' private meeting with Peter to reassure him of complete forgiveness, she said, "Jesus needs to do that for me too." And I replied, "Oh, but He does! Jesus gives reminders of His forgiveness throughout His Word!" Here are a few:

If we confess our sins, He is faithful and just to forgive us our sins and to cleanse us from all unrighteousness. (1 John 1:9)

There is therefore now no condemnation for those who are in Christ Jesus. (Romans 8:1)

As far as the east is from the west, so far does He remove our transgressions from us. (Psalm 103:12)

When you feel weighed down by your guilt, confess your sin and receive the pardon Jesus offers. He has already washed away your sin and shame. Run to Him with the joy of forgiveness.

God's Measure of Success

God doesn't measure our success by our perfection. He invites us to live joyfully forgiven and measured by His grace. Look again at John 21 where Jesus met the disciples at the Sea of Galilee after His resurrection. When the disciples lowered their nets on the right side of the boat at the suggestion of the stranger on the beach and pulled up so many fish they couldn't haul in the net, John recognized the stranger as Jesus. But it was Peter—too impatient to wait for the boat to reach the shore—who jumped in and swam to Jesus. He no longer shrank back in fear, wondering what Jesus might think of him. He was joyfully forgiven!

WHEN WE HAVE FAILED, WE CAN STILL RUN TO JESUS, THE SOURCE OF MERCY AND GRACE.

I love how Paul David Tripp puts this in his devotional *New Morning Mercies*:

> In the face of your failure, you can wallow in guilt and shame, beating yourself up because you did not do better and working hard to hide your failure from God and others. Or in the brokenness and grief of conviction, you can run not away from God but to him. You can run into the light of his holy presence utterly unafraid, filled with the confidence that although he is righteous and you are not, he will not turn you away.[78]

Aren't you thankful that Jesus chose bumbling Peter as a disciple? Through the example of that impulsive disciple, we learn that failure is an opportunity to see our need for grace. We can let go of our need to prove our own strength and lean on Jesus. Through Peter's drive for comparative greatness, we discover that God doesn't define success as being farther up the ladder of earthly achievement than someone else. This frees us from the trap of comparison and allows us to focus on our personal walk with Jesus. And because of Peter's story, we find confidence in the truth that when we have failed, we can still run (or walk or crawl or even swim) to Jesus, the source of mercy and grace.

CHAPTER 8

PAUL: POWERFUL PERSECUTOR

TIMELINE

Joseph	1915 BC
Rahab	1406 BC
David	1010 BC
Jeremiah	628 BC
John the Baptist	1st Century AD
Samaritan Woman	1st Century AD
Peter	1st Century AD
Paul	1st Century AD

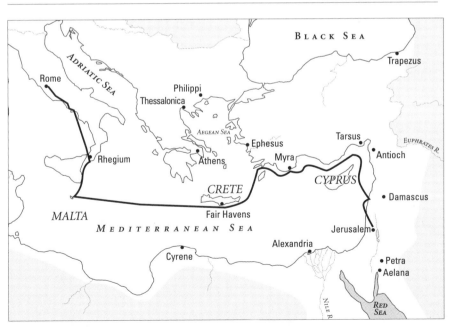

Hanging on to the side of the ship, I brace myself against the wind. Rain pelts my face. Twenty-foot waves plaster me with salt water. I can only see two feet in front of me through the curtain of water.

I squint against the punishing rain and think of the irony that it has taken imprisonment to fulfill my dreams. I never would have guessed I would find myself in this predicament. When we left the island of Crete, a gentle wind propelled our ship, and I anticipated the opportunity to sail to Rome. I had long yearned to spread the Good News of Jesus in the most important city of the Roman Empire.

But not long after leaving Crete, a northeaster attacked the vessel, blowing it farther and farther from land. For the past fourteen days, we have barely clung to life. If God hadn't given me the assurance that I would eventually reach Rome, I would think all was lost.

How could a Jewish boy from Tarsus and Jerusalem end up on a prison boat on his way to trial before Caesar? My studies with Gamaliel prepared me for prominence in our community—not disgrace. My position as an agent of the destruction of the dangerous sect of Jesus followers primed me for success—not failure.

But I wouldn't have it any other way. When Jesus broke through my pride on the road to Damascus, I knew my life would never be the same. Seeing Jesus in His glory convinced me that He was indeed who His followers said He was—the Son of God.

It's possible that I would have had an easier life if I had continued on my path as a Pharisee and persecutor of Christians. Perhaps by now I would have had a seat on the Jewish supreme court, the Sanhedrin.

Instead, others have persecuted *me*. Angry Jews have whipped me. Roman authorities have beaten me. I've endured the rejection of my fellow Jews and imprisonment by the Gentiles.

What's that? I hear the sailors shouting, "Land!" But as hope swells and dawn breaks, the ship has run aground against a reef. Powerful surf smashes this well-built vessel like it's a little bundle of sticks.

Through the wind, we barely hear the centurion shout, "Jump overboard! Grab a plank! Swim to shore!"

As I target a piece of the ship floating in the churning sea and prepare to leap toward it, I wonder what adventure God has for me now. All I know for certain is that it's part of the great success story of my life: knowing Jesus.

KEY VERSE

But He said to me, "My grace is sufficient for you, for My power is made perfect in weakness." Therefore I will boast all the more gladly of my weaknesses, so that the power of Christ may rest upon me. (2 Corinthians 12:9)

In the world of athletics, success is measured in speed and strength. The gold medal goes to the one who can jump the highest or run the fastest. Officials award the trophy to the team that scores the most points. The world applauds those who win and forgets about those who lose.

Paul often compared the Christian life to a race. He told the Christians in Corinth, "Do you not know that in a race all the runners run, but only one receives the prize? So run that you may obtain it" (1 Corinthians 9:24). Of his own life he said, "I press on toward the goal for the prize of the upward call of God in Christ Jesus" (Philippians 3:14). But as we examine Paul's life, we discover that God defines winning very differently than any Olympic committee does.

SETTING THE SCENE

Probably about the same time that young Peter sat beside his father on a fishing boat on the Sea of Galilee, the apostle Paul was born in the city of Tarsus. Paul started out as Saul, born to a Jewish family in a bustling metropolis in the Cilician province of Asia Minor (now part of the nation of Turkey). Near a busy seaport on the Mediterranean Sea and a passage through the Taurus Mountains, Tarsus was a popular stop for traders going east to the Orient or west to Rome.[79]

Paul grew up in a family of devout Jews. In his Letter to the Philippians, he described himself as a "Hebrew of Hebrews" (Philippians 3:5), meaning there were no non-Jews in his lineage.[80] The term *Hebrew* distinguished traditional Jews, who preserved the Aramaic language and used the Hebrew Bible, from Hellenists, who didn't know Aramaic and used the Septuagint (a Greek translation of the Old Testament).[81] Because Paul's family lived in such a diverse city, he probably spoke not only Aramaic but also Greek, the language of commerce, and Latin, the official language of the Romans.

We don't know how long Saul stayed in Tarsus. In Acts 22:3, he told a crowd in Jerusalem, "I am a Jew, born in Tarsus in Cilicia, but brought up in this city, educated at the feet of Gamaliel according to the strict manner of the law of our fathers, being zealous for God as all of you are this day." Some time after Saul was born, his family moved to Jerusalem and made sure their son had the best Jewish education with one of the most respected teachers of Judaism. Probably starting at age thirteen, Paul sat at the feet of the esteemed rabbi Gamaliel and learned how to examine a text of the Hebrew Scriptures from the viewpoint of generations of rabbis.[82] He grew up on a steady diet of God's Word.

PRIMED FOR SUCCESS

No doubt about it. Saul of Tarsus was primed for success in his Jewish world. He later described his background to King Agrippa:

> My manner of life from my youth, spent from the beginning among my own nation and in Jerusalem, is known by all the Jews. They have known for a long time, if they are willing to testify, that according to the strictest party of our religion I have lived as a Pharisee. (Acts 26:4–5)

Not merely a devout Jew, Saul lived as one of the strictest followers of Judaism—a Pharisee. The main Jewish sect of Saul's day, the Pharisees desired to live in God's favor by setting themselves apart from the Gentiles.[83] They not only aimed to obey all of God's laws in the Torah but also added many more regulations intended to clarify those original commandments. I can imagine a young, earnest Saul diligently learning all those rules and striving to follow them all. To win the race for Jewish virtue, he would have to excel in obedience.

When Saul became a grown man, we see his zeal for his faith. He proved his fervor by getting rid of people who worshiped false gods. In his mind, this included followers of Jesus. Since most of us come to Saul's story with a Gentile mindset, his persecution of Christians seems unthinkable. But as an ardent Jew, he thought he was stamping out fires of false religion.

We first read about Saul's persecution of Christians in the stoning of Stephen in Acts 7. The Jews stoned Stephen to death on false charges of desecrating the temple. But before they threw the first stone, they "laid down their garments at the feet of a young man named Saul" (Acts 7:58).

Saul's zeal for the Jewish faith and determination to eradicate opposition to it appears to have made him the chief persecutor of Christians.[84] Acts 8:3 tells of his tireless efforts: "Saul was ravaging the church, and entering house after house, he dragged off men and women and committed them to prison."

Because of Saul's persistent persecution, many Christians fled Jerusalem and settled in other cities where they continued to share the Good News of Jesus. Instead of eliminating the Jesus followers, Saul's efforts had resulted in their multiplication! Of course, he couldn't stand this, so "Saul, still breathing threats and murder against the disciples of the Lord, went to the high priest and asked him

IF THE LIFE OF JUDAISM WERE A RACE, SAUL WOULD HAVE WON A GOLD MEDAL.

for letters to the synagogues at Damascus, so that if he found any belonging to the Way, men or women, he might bring them bound to Jerusalem"

(Acts 9:1–2). Notice that Saul went to the high priest for permission for his mission. Tormenting Christians had become an official act of the Sanhedrin, the Jewish supreme court.

Saul was on his way to becoming important in the world of Judaism. He was descended from a respected Jewish family and had studied with the most revered rabbi. He meticulously obeyed all of the Jewish laws and strove for perfection in following the Commandments. He became a member of the strict sect of the Pharisees and had audience with the high priest. His zeal led him to work harder and harder. If the life of Judaism were a race, Saul would have won a gold medal.

PHARISEES

In Acts 26, Paul talks about his former life as a Pharisee. The term *Pharisee* means "separate." It described the attempt of this strict sect to separate themselves from ritual uncleanness. Because previous intermingling of Yahweh worship with idol worship had landed the Israelites in Babylonian captivity, the Pharisees aimed for complete religious purity. To obtain this, they tried to clarify God's original laws with hundreds of additional rules.

For instance, God's Law commanded the Jews to keep the Sabbath holy. God gave His people a day of rest each week. No work. To clarify what "work" meant, the Pharisees added rules that prescribed how many steps a person could take and how many letters he could write on a Sabbath.[85] Other Sabbath laws prohibited looking in a mirror and lighting a candle.[86]

Weakness and Anonymity

But everything changed on the way to Damascus. Saul and his party were traveling the 135 miles to the Syrian city when someone halted his journey:

Now as he went on his way, he approached Damascus, and

suddenly a light from heaven shone around him. And falling to the ground, he heard a voice saying to him, "Saul, Saul, why are you persecuting Me?" And he said, "Who are You, Lord?" And He said, "I am Jesus, whom you are persecuting. But rise and enter the city, and you will be told what you are to do." The men who were traveling with him stood speechless, hearing the voice but seeing no one. Saul rose from the ground, and although his eyes were opened, he saw nothing. So they led him by the hand and brought him into Damascus. And for three days he was without sight, and neither ate nor drank. (Acts 9:3–9)

Suddenly, the strong, confident Saul became weak and blind. Instead of leading the drive to arrest Christians in Damascus, he was led into the city to wait in darkness.

On the third day, God sent faithful Ananias to help Saul. He laid hands on Saul and prayed for him. Immediately "something like scales fell from his eyes, and he regained his sight" (Acts 9:18). Saul got up and was baptized.

His transformation amazed everyone. Instead of breathing murderous threats against Jesus followers, he started proclaiming Jesus as the Son of God (Acts 9:20). This change from persecutor to proclaimer didn't please most of the Jews, and they plotted to kill him. When the Jesus followers heard of the plot, they helped Saul to escape by lowering him in a basket through an opening in the city wall. The great and mighty Saul, who once sought attention, now needed to avoid attention entirely and escape.

Saul's descent into weakness and anonymity continued as he fled to Arabia (Galatians 1:17), where he spent three years alone,[87] and then to Damascus before returning to Jerusalem. This homecoming looked nothing like the one Saul had envisioned three years earlier. Instead of triumphantly returning to applause and approval from the Jewish power brokers, he came back to rejection and avoidance. Former acquaintances shunned him. And the disciples of Jesus feared him (Acts 9:26). Then a man named

GOD SEEMS TO HAVE USED A TIME OF ANONYMITY AND WEAKNESS IN PAUL'S LIFE TO SHAPE AND FORM HIM AS HIS CHOSEN INSTRUMENT.

Barnabas persuaded the apostles that Saul had truly seen the Lord and had genuinely experienced a conversion. The Christians then accepted Saul. But again, he needed rescue from a Jewish murder plot. To save him, the believers smuggled Saul to the seaport of Caesarea and put him on a boat to Tarsus. We hear no more about God's messenger to the Gentiles for six to seven years.

Finally, we learn that Barnabas traveled to Antioch to check on the Christians there and remembered Saul. Barnabas journeyed north to Tarsus to meet Saul and bring him back to Antioch, where "they met with the church and taught a great many people" (Acts 11:26). Following the instructions of the Holy Spirit, the Antioch Christians sent Saul and Barnabas on a missionary journey. It's on this first journey that Scripture begins to refer to Saul as Paul (Acts 13:9).

SAUL TO PAUL

The apostle Paul began life as Saul of Tarsus. His parents, who belonged to the tribe of Benjamin, gave their son the royal name of one of the most famous Benjamites, King Saul. In his early years, Saul of Tarsus attempted to live up to the greatness of that name as he pursued perfection according to the Law and prominence in the Jewish culture.

But after Saul met Jesus and began his missionary journeys to spread the Good News about the Messiah, he changed his name to Paul—a Greek name. Commentators speculate about the change. Did he use the name Paul because it was more common in the non-Jewish world? Did he, like many Roman citizens, have two names and switch between them according to the situation? Or did he purposely choose Paul, which comes from the Greek adjective for "small or little," as a sign of his humility?[88]

Ten years after God dramatically called Paul as His chosen instrument to the Gentiles (Acts 9:15), he finally began his work. We might think God wasted time in not using Paul sooner, but God's timing is always perfect. Just as when Joseph spent time in prison before becoming second-in-command in Egypt, and David lived for years in the wilderness before ascending to the throne, God seems to have used a time of anonymity and weakness in Paul's life to shape and form him as His chosen instrument.

Weakness = Success

Saul began his life striving to prove himself through obedience to God's laws and loyalty to the Jewish leaders of his day, but Paul became a success when God taught him the power of weakness. On paper, Paul's missionary journeys may look like a series of triumphs. The first trip took Paul and Barnabas to Cyprus and Galatia. Next, Paul traveled with Silas to Troas, Macedonia, Greece, and Ephesus. On his third journey, he went to Syrian Antioch, Ephesus, Macedonia, Achaia, Troas, Melitas, and Rhodes. Travel meant hiking over mountain passes and sailing on rough seas. Plus, Paul didn't always receive a warm welcome. He experienced imprisonment, beatings, and lashings. He miraculously survived a stoning and three shipwrecks. Robbers, Gentiles, and his own people posed constant threats. Hunger and thirst, cold and exposure, accompanied him.

Before Paul met Jesus, he was the one putting people in jail, participating in stonings, and administering punishments. Then, as a follower of Jesus, Paul *received* mistreatment and abuse. Before, Paul had enjoyed a position of strength and authority. Now, he was in a position of continual weakness. As if that wasn't enough, Paul also endured a particularly painful trial. The ordeal came at about the same time he experienced a wonderful vision, or taste, of heaven. As God blessed Paul with extraordinary revelations, He allowed the trial to keep him from becoming prideful:

> So to keep me from becoming conceited because of the surpassing greatness of the revelations, a thorn was given me in the flesh, a messenger of Satan to harass me, to keep me from becoming conceited. (2 Corinthians 12:7)

Commentators speculate about this "thorn," suggesting "eye misery, headaches, malaria, ear trouble, sciatica, rheumatism, Malta fever, leprosy, some nervous disorder, hysteria, or melancholy, epilepsy."[89] Whatever the malady, like a deeply imbedded thorn, it wouldn't go away. Paul goes on:

> Three times I pleaded with the Lord about this, that it should leave me. But He said to me, "My grace is sufficient for you, for My power is made perfect in weakness." Therefore I will boast all the more gladly of my weaknesses, so that the power of Christ may rest upon me. For the sake of Christ, then, I am content with weaknesses, insults, hardships, persecutions, and calamities. For when I am weak, then I am strong. (2 Corinthians 12:8–10)

Paul did have great accomplishments to boast about. Imagine if someone today achieved what he did: traveling worldwide, planting churches among people who had never heard of Jesus, writing thirteen definitive and influential books on faith. Christians everywhere would praise and applaud this kind of success. Who wouldn't boast a little?

But what does Paul boast about? His weaknesses. Paul's experiences taught him that success doesn't come through achievement. It comes through human weakness that requires reliance on the strength of God alone. More weakness makes more room for God's power.

Perhaps before the encounter with Christ, Saul saw himself as the capable runner, competing not in the Greek Olympics but in the Jewish race for purity and power. The Usain Bolt of the Jewish world, he had the talent to go far, the training to give him an edge, and the determination to make it happen.

But after meeting Jesus, after ten years in anonymity, after beatings and imprisonments, after a thorn that wouldn't go away, Paul realized his weakness without Christ. Instead of emulating Usain Bolt, he was more like Rick Hoyt. Maybe you've heard about him. Rick has completed many marathons—but not under his own power. Born with cerebral palsy, Rick cannot take even one step on his own. But in 1977, Rick asked his father, Dick, if they could run in a race together that would benefit a lacrosse player at Rick's school who had become paralyzed. Dick couldn't say no. So although he wasn't a runner, Dick pushed Rick in his wheelchair for the entire five-mile race. After that first competition, Rick typed on his computer, "Dad, when I'm running it feels like my disability disappears," and Team Hoyt was born. Dick began training so he and his son could compete together. From 1977 to 2014, they completed 72 marathons and 255 triathlons. Rick ran races under his father's power.[90]

SUCCESS DOESN'T COME THROUGH ACHIEVEMENT. IT COMES THROUGH RELIANCE ON THE STRENGTH OF GOD.

That's exactly how we need to run the Christian race to eternity—under our Father's power. But often we need to experience weakness before we willingly get into the wheelchair and allow the strength of Christ to propel us. It took years of anonymity and a persistent thorn to get Paul to the point where he could say, "When I am weak, then I am strong" (2 Corinthians 12:10). R. C. H. Lenski writes about God's power in our lives:

> This power works and does things in us. It has much to do. When it has brought us to the point where we are utter weakness, its task is finished. It has then shaped us into a perfect tool for itself. As long as we as sinners imagine that *we* still have some power we are unfit instruments for the Lord's hands; he still has to work on us before he can work properly through us.[91]

God asks us to acknowledge our weakness—to get into that wheelchair so His power can propel us to victory. As soon as we get out of the chair, we put ourselves at a disadvantage because, on our own, we are spiritually disabled. But when we trust in Jesus, our disability disappears. Can we come to the point where we, like Paul, rejoice in weakness, in seeming failure, simply because it means an opportunity to rely even more on the grace of God?

WHEN YOU FEEL WEAK

As we adopt the new paradigm that weakness can actually lead to success in God's kingdom, we can learn specific ways to apply that perspective. In another passage in which Paul talks about abandoning boasting in himself and instead relying on Christ, I see three lessons about success.

Striving for worldly success can be a detriment to our spiritual success. Paul writes:

> If anyone else thinks he has reason for confidence in the flesh, I have more: circumcised on the eighth day, of the people of Israel, of the tribe of Benjamin, a Hebrew of Hebrews; as to the law, a Pharisee; as to zeal, a persecutor of the church; as to righteousness under the law, blameless. But whatever gain I had, I counted as loss for the sake of Christ. (Philippians 3:4b–7)

Before Saul met Christ, he determined to obey God's Law and prove his zeal for God by persecuting people he thought violated that Law. In Galatians, Paul writes, "I was advancing in Judaism beyond many of my own age among my people, so extremely zealous was I for the traditions of my fathers" (Galatians 1:14). Paul did his best to reach the top rank in his Jewish circle.

But after Paul met Jesus, he realized all that striving and posturing was unnecessary because we are saved by *grace* through faith, not by our own efforts. And even more than deeming them unnecessary, he viewed his background, striving, and achievements as loss. *Zemia*, the Greek word translated "loss," means not only "loss" but "detriment." The success Paul aimed for in his early life damaged his relationship with God because it caused him to rely on himself instead of on God's mercy.

Sometimes God grants success in this world and we can rejoice in it. But let's accept that success with caution, viewing it as a potential liability to our spiritual life. When we fail or achieve less than we hoped for, can we look at that as an advantage? Or as a blessing because it forces us to lean a little more on God's grace?

Success is knowing Christ. Paul goes on in Philippians 3:

> Indeed, I count everything as loss because of the surpassing worth of knowing Christ Jesus my Lord. For His sake I have suffered the loss of all things and count them as rubbish, in order that I may gain Christ and be found in Him, not having a righteousness of my own that comes from the law, but that which comes through faith in Christ, the righteousness from God that depends on faith. (Philippians 3:8–9)

Paul now writes that he considers *everything* as a loss or detriment. Since Paul wrote this letter while imprisoned (see Philippians 1:7), he probably did lose nearly everything. He lost the freedom to go where he wanted, the liberty to engage in his profession of preaching, and his ability to provide for himself, making him dependent on friends for food and other necessities. Yet he gained the one thing that truly matters: knowing Christ Jesus. Knowing He is the only way to eternal success. Knowing He is the only means to true peace here on earth. Knowing He is the way to living a grace-filled life even in the midst of pain and loss.

THE SUCCESS OF KNOWING CHRIST JESUS

The Greek word for "knowledge," *gnosis*, implies more than an intellectual apprehension. It indicates heart knowledge.[92] The *Amplified Bible* expands the idea of this word as "progressively becoming more deeply *and* intimately acquainted with Him [of perceiving and recognizing and understanding Him more fully and clearly]" (Philippians 3:8, *AMP*). According to Paul, achievement and worldly prominence didn't matter. To him, success meant increasingly understanding and knowing Christ.

Success is not perfection but transformation. Paul writes:

> Not that I have already obtained this or am already perfect, but
> I press on to make it my own, because Christ Jesus has made
> me His own. Brothers, I do not consider that I have made it
> my own. But one thing I do: forgetting what lies behind and
> straining forward to what lies ahead, I press on toward the
> goal for the prize of the upward call of God in Christ Jesus.
> (Philippians 3:12–14)

Paul had not yet achieved perfection. The Greek word *teleioo* means
"completeness or attaining a goal." After God has redeemed us, He contin-
ues to *complete* the task of sanctification—of making us holy and Christlike. While this task can't be completed until heaven, Paul pressed toward
it "because Christ Jesus has made me His own."

WE PURSUE THE GOAL OF BECOMING MORE CHRISTLIKE BECAUSE WE ALREADY BELONG TO HIM.

What a beautiful thought. We don't have to
press on toward perfection to earn our salvation.
Christ has already done that. But we pursue the
goal of becoming more Christlike because we already belong to Him.

Paul presses on and strains forward. Like a runner desperate for a gold medal, he stretches toward
"the prize of the upward call of God in Christ Jesus"
(Philippians 3:14). He strives not to prove himself but to arrive successfully
at the finish line of heaven looking less like the self-confident Pharisee he
was on the way to Damascus and more like the Savior who took hold of
him on that road.

God's Measure of Success

In this world, we will never be perfect or be exactly like Christ, but to
Paul, a successful life meant pursuing that goal. Author David Paul Tripp
challenges readers to have that view of success:

You're going to hunger for some success in life. May you hunger for the complete success of the Gospel in your heart.[93]

SIGN UP FOR THE MARATHON WON BY GETTING INTO THE WHEELCHAIR AND ALLOWING THE FATHER TO PUSH YOU TO THE FINISH LINE.

What kind of race are you running? A sprint to the top of your company? A 5K to win that prestigious award? A marathon to get your child into that top college?

Paul urges us to abandon those contests. God doesn't measure success by how fast or far we can run on our own or how much we can do in our own strength. Success comes when we admit our weakness and depend on the power of the Lord.

So sign up for the race for the success of God's grace in your heart. The 5K of thankfulness for the Holy Spirit's continual, sanctifying work through Word and Sacrament. The marathon won by getting into the wheelchair and allowing the Father to push you to the finish line.

EPILOGUE

All of my life I have searched for success. Obviously, most people don't aim for failure. But from a young age, I had an internal success meter that measured every success or failure I experienced. I believed the number on my success meter determined how far I would go in life. A 10 meant I was going places; my life mattered. A 2 meant I would never amount to anything; I was worthless.

As a young child, A's on my report card bumped the success meter to a 10. Messing up my piano piece at my lesson scored a 3. Later, having my teaching schedule filled with talented piano students measured a 9, but a student quitting brought the meter to 2. The success meter shot to 10 when I published a new book but sank to 4 when another author had more readers at her book-signing table. And with every rise or fall of my success gauge, my self-esteem soared or plummeted.

But in the past few years, time in God's Word has convinced me that my internal success meter has been measuring the wrong things. God gauges success much differently than the world around me does. I decided to dig deeper into Scripture to discover exactly what God's success meter measures. The result? This book.

In *Measured by Grace*, you and I have studied eight success stories recorded in the Bible. Joseph's life taught us that God measures success in faithfulness in the small things. Rahab's story demonstrated that God doesn't gauge our success according to our qualifications. In David's biography, we saw that a monumental failure doesn't bar us from going to God for grace. We learned from Jeremiah that God doesn't measure our success according to the size of our audience.

John the Baptist embraced God's definition of success by becoming less. The story of the woman at the well taught us that even multiple failures don't exclude us from triumph in God's kingdom. Peter taught us that even when we fail big-time, we can still run to Jesus. And Paul's life demonstrates the truth that God measures us a 10 on His success meter when our weakness makes us a 1.

But we have one more story to examine. The greatest success story of all reiterates all we have learned about how the Lord measures success. Oh, this person didn't start out looking like a winner. Born in a barn to a poor, insignificant couple, He lived in obscurity for thirty years and trained as a lowly carpenter. When He began His career, He started by choosing twelve misfits as assistants. Although He demonstrated miraculous skills, He shunned publicity. He disguised the fact that He descended from royalty and instead assumed the role of a servant. When forced to face false charges in court, He didn't try to defend Himself but willingly took an unjust punishment and died a criminal's death.

The greatest success story of all time certainly looked like a failure.

But Jesus willingly took the guise of failure in order to achieve victory for us. The apostle Paul talks about Christ's attitude toward success:

> Have this mind among yourselves, which is yours in Christ Jesus, who, though He was in the form of God, did not count equality with God a thing to be grasped, but emptied Himself, by taking the form of a servant, being born in the likeness of men. And being found in human form, He humbled Himself by becoming obedient to the point of death, even death on a cross. (Philippians 2:5–8)

Although Jesus deserved royal treatment, He lived simply—so we could live as His royal priesthood. Without praise or acclaim, He lived a perfect life—because He knew we couldn't. He willingly looked like a dismal failure on a cross of shame—so we could experience the ultimate success of a relationship with Him.

To most people of His day, Jesus' life did not appear successful. Yet He achieved the greatest feat possible—defeating death and Satan by dying for the sins of the world and rising from the dead. His triumph ensures that each of our lives can have a rags-to-riches ending. Although we began in the rags of sin, through God's gift of faith in Jesus, we can all have the riches of heaven.

And not only do we have a guaranteed happy ending, but we can live the rest of our journeys here without a false success meter determining our worth. The prophet Isaiah says:

> Because you are precious in My eyes,
>> and honored, and I love you,
> I give men in return for you,
>> peoples in exchange for your life. (Isaiah 43:4)

Listen. God deems you precious. Period. Your worth in His eyes does not depend on your accomplishments. The Lord declares you honored. His regard for you doesn't fluctuate with how much you achieve. The Father loves you. And this everlasting, unchanging love doesn't increase when you succeed or diminish when you fail. He loves you so much that He gave His Son in return for you. He bases His view of you exclusively on the truth that Jesus took your place on the cross.

So join me in living free from the constant search for validation through accomplishment. Free from an unquenchable desire to make a name for ourselves. Free from all-consuming ambitions. Free from an internal success meter that falsely measures our merit.

Instead, rest in the sacred worth you have as a child of the heavenly Father. Rejoice that God values you so much that He gave His only Son for you. Live measured by grace.

STUDY GUIDE

I invite you to learn more about God's grace by going deeper into Scripture. Read the stories of the biblical characters we've studied straight from God's Word. The study questions that follow will help you focus on the Lord's lessons about failure and success. I have organized the questions in levels according to the time it takes to complete them.

- **Level 1: Reflect on the Reading.** If you have only fifteen minutes, complete this section. These questions will help you reflect on the chapter's lessons and make them more personal. If you are doing the study in a group, these questions will start conversation flowing.

- **Level 2: Dig into the Word.** If you have more time, dive deeper into the Word by reading the Bible story of each character and answering questions designed to help you study the biblical narrative.

- **Level 3: Apply the Word to Your Life.** Here you'll discover how to apply the lessons of each biblical character to your everyday life.

- **Level 4: Create a Project.** To help you internalize what you have learned, here are some practical exercises and hands-on activities. To encourage your heart, I've also included a playlist of music. You can find recordings of these songs online. If you are doing this study in a group, consider doing the activities together as people arrive for the study. The suggested songs could be playing in the background. Perhaps one member of the group could take charge of getting materials for these projects and another could be responsible for obtaining the playlist for the session.

Questions and answers referring to the biblical text are based on the English Standard Version (ESV) translation of the Bible.

Chapter 1

Joseph: Detoured Dreamer

Reflect on the Reading

1. Describe what first comes to mind when you think of a successful person.

   Enjoys a Good Life!

2. In the chapter, we read, "God measures our success based on our dependence on Him." How does this scale of success differ from the world's scale?

   Great lee!

3. Have you known someone who the world might not define as successful but who made an impact on his or her corner of the world? Describe that person.

   My Grandmother.

4. What is your biggest takeaway from this chapter?

   Be Faithful.

Dig into the Word

Joseph's story spans Genesis 37–50. You may want to read the whole account of his life, but to focus on our topic of success and failure, we concentrate on Genesis 39.

When studying a biblical story, it can be helpful to look for certain features of the account to understand it better. Let's examine four features of the Joseph narrative in Genesis 39 and make some discoveries.

1. **Repeated words and phrases.** Whenever we see repeated words or phrases in a biblical narrative, we should pay attention. These words usually indicate a major theme or lesson to learn.[94] What words and phrases do you see in Genesis 39? Use the chart below to record your findings. (I did one phrase for you, as an example.)

Word or Phrase	Verses Where These Appear
"The LORD was with Joseph."	Genesis 39:2, 3, 21
Showed Him Stedfast Love	39.21
Made what He did succeed	" 39-23
Showed Him Kindness	39.21
He pospered -	39-21
Success in all He did	39-23
Blessed the household	39-5

Looking at these repeated words and phrases, summarize some of the themes of this chapter.

2. **Actions.** Especially when the Bible records a Bible character performing a similar action more than once, it may do so to teach us something about his or her personality or integrity.[95]

   a. Write down activities that Joseph did more than once in Genesis 39.

   All of the above

   b. What do these reveal about his character?

   He was Faithful to God

3. **Dialogue.** The first time a person speaks in Scripture or even in a certain scene often reveals something about his or her character.[96]

a. What does Joseph say the first time he speaks in Genesis 39? *- 9 -*

b. What does this reveal about his character?

He was true to God

4. **Narration.** Now look at the narration of the story (everything but the dialogue). What does the biblical narrator reveal about the motives and feelings of the following people in this chapter?[97]

a. Potiphar *He trusted Joseph !*

b. Potiphar's wife *She tempted Him.*

c. The jailer *Trusted Joseph*

d. Joseph *- Was true to God.*

Remember that two purposes of Joseph's story are to demonstrate the providence of God and to teach us how God defines success. How did the narrator help us understand these better?

APPLY THE WORD TO YOUR LIFE

Joseph's story teaches us that God doesn't define success in terms of impressive titles or humongous homes. In God's eyes, success means relying on Him to complete the work He has given us—whether that work seems trivial or important in our eyes. Still, we don't like to feel small when we live in a world that applauds big. In this chapter, we examined a few suggestions for living small in a big world. I've included these principles below. Below each, write a few specific ways to practice these principles in your own life. For instance, for the first one, I could write, "Even if only a few people show up for church, I will sing my solo like I'm singing it for Jesus."

a. Do your best in whatever position you find yourself.

Be Happy & Enjoy Life as it is Given to you!

b. Learn humility and servanthood.

c. Realize real success comes from God.

d. Lean on God's presence and steadfast love.

Remember He is always there for you!

CREATE A PROJECT

1. Using the word *success*, construct an acronym. Choose words
    that reflect the way God defines success and that start with
    each of the letters of the word *success*. I did the first one.

    Small in the eyes of the world

    U *using my life to serve other*

    C *aring about family + friends*

    C

    E *njoy all that the Lord has given me*

    S

    S *haring my faith with others*

2. Throughout this book, we explore spiritual disciplines that
    help us achieve a success that God applauds. In Joseph's life,
    we see that God purposely gave Joseph positions of service
    to teach him humility. Life as a servant isn't the success the
    world notices, but God will see each seemingly insignificant,
    selfless act done in faith.

    This week, look for opportunities to serve. You might take
    on a new volunteer position, working at a food pantry or
    literacy center. But you don't have to think big. Hold open
    a door for someone. Shovel a neighbor's driveway. Mentor
    someone at your workplace. Put down your phone and help
    your child with his or her homework. Make your husband's
    favorite dessert. In the space below, brainstorm a couple of
    ideas you could do today.

3. Music can touch our hearts and help us remember the prin-
    ciples we have learned. Consider singing or listening to "He
    Knows My Name" by Francesca Battistelli or "Lift My Life
    Up" by Unspoken. Sing "Come unto Me, Ye Weary" (*LSB*
    684) or "Love Divine, All Loves Excelling" (*LSB* 700).

Chapter 2

Rahab: Risqué Romancer

Reflect on the Reading

1. Place a mark on the line below indicating how qualified for success you feel right now.

I feel very
qualified
to succeed.

I don't feel at
all qualified
to succeed.

What factors made you place your mark there?
Your past successes or failures? Your strengths or perceived imperfections? Comments from other people?

God is always there for me!

2. Rahab's faith in the one true God changed her life and brought success to her and the Israelites. The world more often tells us to believe in ourselves. Where do you see this message pushed in advertisements, books, movies, social media memes, and so forth?

3. When you read "Success in God's kingdom does not depend on our qualifications," what is your first reaction? How does this truth free you? *It's not how successful we are But How Faithful*

4. What is your biggest takeaway from this chapter?
Trust in the Faith.

Dig into the Word

Read Rahab's story as it appears in Joshua 2 and 6. (Other important events related to the fall of Jericho happen in chapters 3–5. You may want to read these also.) As you read, keep an eye out for the important elements of a biblical narrative.

1. a. **Repeated words and phrases.** Record any words or phrases you see repeated in Joshua 2. I did one for you.

Word or Phrase	Verses Where These Appear
"the Lord"	Joshua 2:9, 10, 11, 12, 14
Pervsue Pervsuers	*7- 16-22*
Fear - nospirit -	*9-11*
melt -	*9-11-24*
heard	*18-11*
guiltless -	*17 -19-20*
Scarlet cord	*18-21*

   b. Looking at the words and phrases, summarize some of the themes of the chapter.

2. **Actions.** James 2:25 praises Rahab's faith in action. What actions do you see in Joshua 2 that display her faith in Yahweh?
   Housing the spies -

3. **Dialogue.** a. The first time Scripture records Rahab's words, she speaks to the king's men in Joshua 2:4–5. As you read these verses, consider what her words reveal about her character. *Brave*

b. The longest recorded prose speech of any woman in the Bible is Rahab's words to the Israelite spies in Joshua 2:8–13.[98] What does this speech reveal about her character?

Faith + Family —

c. In the first speech, Rahab lies to the soldiers; in the second, she expresses faith in God. How do you reconcile these two conflicting sides of her character?

4. **Narration.** Now look at the narration—the words not in dialogue. What does the biblical narrator reveal about the character of these people in Joshua 2 and 6?

a. The Israelite spies *trusting*

b. The people of Jericho *Afraid*

c. Joshua *obiedant to the Lord.*

d. Rahab *Faithful —*

APPLY THE WORD TO YOUR LIFE

1. The narrator often mentions Rahab's profession.

a. How many times do you see the word *prostitute* in Joshua 2 and 6? *4+*

b. Why do you think the Bible keeps mentioning the fact that Rahab was a prostitute?

So we realize that God saves all! if possible

2. If someone wrote a story about you and used a word or phrase to describe you, what would it be? (My biographer might write, "Sharla, the klutz" or "Sharla, the last chosen in all sports.")

_____, the _____
Your Name   Description

3. God chose Rahab despite her faults. He redeemed her and transformed her from Rahab, the prostitute, to Rahab, the spy saver. How do you see God already transforming you from the description above into someone He loves and uses to glorify His name?

4. Rahab became not only Rahab, the spy saver, but also Rahab, the ancestor of Jesus! We won't know the full extent of our faithful actions until we reach heaven. But it might be eye-opening to discover our own family trees of faith.

Start by asking yourself, "Who played an instrumental role in leading me to Jesus or helping me grow in faith?" It might be a parent, a Sunday School teacher, a youth group leader, a friend, an author. Write the name here:

My Parents - and Hand parents

If possible, contact that person and ask him or her the same question. Write that name here:

_____

If possible, ask person number 1 to ask person number 2 the same question. See how far you can construct the family tree of your faith. List any more names here:

CREATE A PROJECT

1. In this chapter, we learned that the scarlet thread, or cord, that hung from Rahab's window and saved her and her family can picture Christ's scarlet blood that saved you and me. We also discovered that *tiqvâ*, the word translated as "thread" or "line," can also mean "hope" or "expectation."

    Consider making a bookmark out of scarlet thread to remind you of the hope we have because of Jesus' blood. For a fancier bookmark, you could photocopy the graphic on the right, color it as you like, then glue or tape a red ribbon to the back.

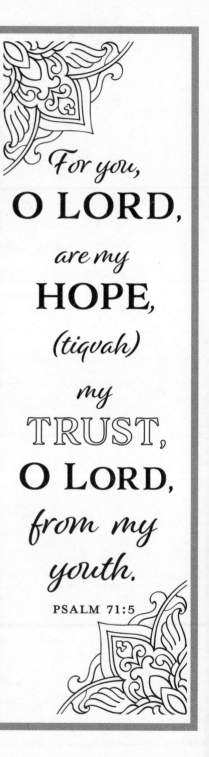

For you,
O LORD,
are my
HOPE,
(tiqvah)
my
TRUST,
O LORD,
from my
youth.

PSALM 71:5

2. Rahab's faith in a big God convinced her to side with the Israelites instead of her own people. She proclaimed, "The LORD your God, He is God in the heavens above and on the earth beneath" (Joshua 2:11). The spiritual discipline of worshiping our almighty God can help us remember that success does not depend on our qualifications but on God's power. Today spend some time praising God for His might and strength. You might use one or more of the following psalms to guide your worship: Psalm 29, 47, 93, 121.

3. You could also use music to direct your worship. Consider singing "How Firm a Foundation" (*LSB* 728) or "O God, Our Help in Ages Past" (*LSB* 733). Or listen to "Our God" by Chris Tomlin or "Jericho" by Andrew Ripp.

CHAPTER 3

DAVID: SUPERSIZE SINNER

REFLECT ON THE READING

1. When you experience failure, do you worry about how God sees you?

2. Why do you think God thought of David as "a man after His own heart" despite David's many failings? Do you think this implies a continual and glorious straining for the things of God, or is it more descriptive of the flavor of David's life at his most faithful?

3. Describe your reaction to this quote from the chapter: "To be counted as a woman after God's own heart, I don't need to be perfect—just forgiven!"

4. What is your biggest takeaway from this chapter?

God is a forgiving God.

DIG INTO THE WORD

We find David's story in 1 Samuel 16–31, 2 Samuel 1–24, 1 Kings 1–2, and 1 Chronicles 11–29. When you have time, I encourage you to read the entire account of his life, but for now let's concentrate on the story of David's giant success. You may have heard the story of David and Goliath many times, but ask the Holy Spirit to give you fresh eyes as you read 1 Samuel 17. Then answer these questions about the four important elements of a biblical narrative.

1. **Repeated words and phrases.** a. Complete this chart by reading these verses and noting how they describe David.

Verse	Description of David
1 Samuel 17:14	*Youngest*
1 Samuel 17:33	*A Boy*
1 Samuel 17:42	*Boy ruddy & handsome*
1 Samuel 17:55	*Young man*

b. What descriptive word do you see repeated? Why do you think this word is repeated so often?

Young.

2. **Actions.** Now look at David's actions in this chapter. Write what he did and what each action demonstrates about his character. I've done the first one for you.

Verse	Action	What the Action Reveals about David's Character
1 Samuel 17:15	David went back and forth from playing the harp for King Saul to tending the sheep.	Even after having "royal duties," David didn't consider himself too important to do the humble work of tending the sheep.
1 Samuel 17:17–20	*Take the food to those fighting*	*He wasn't afraid*
1 Samuel 17:38–39	*Dress him to fight - But*	*He removed it & took a staff & 5 stones & a sling.*
1 Samuel 17:40	*You come with men & weapons*	*I come with God!*
1 Samuel 17:48–51	*He came with stone + sling*	*He killed Goliath + cut off his head*

3. **Dialogue.** a. As you read the following verses, write down who David spoke to and what you think those words reveal about David. Pay special attention to 1 Samuel 17:26, as these are David's first recorded words in Scripture. Remember that the first time a person speaks in Scripture often discloses something important about his or her character.

Verse	Who David Spoke To	What David's Words Reveal about His Character
1 Samuel 17:26	*Spoke Men there to fight –*	*No-fear*
1 Samuel 17:29	*v↓*	
1 Samuel 17:32–37	*I will kill Saul Golitha*	*The Lord will be with me*
1 Samuel 17:45–47	*Pellistine Go litha*	*I come with the Lord*

b. How would you summarize David's character based on what you discovered from his actions and dialogue?

Strong Faith in God.

c. From your knowledge of David's life, how do you see these characteristics play out in the rest of his story?

4. **Narration.** Now look at the narration of the story (everything but the dialogue). What does the biblical narrator reveal about the motives and feelings of the following people in this chapter?

a. Goliath (1 Samuel 17:3–10)

Big Mean Strong –

b. The Israelite soldiers (1 Samuel 17:11, 20–24)

c. Saul (1 Samuel 17:38, 55)

Fear

APPLY THE WORD TO YOUR LIFE

When we examined David's successes and his failures, we saw some patterns in behavior. Below are the patterns we discovered in his success against Goliath. For each of David's actions, write a general principle you can use to be successful in God's eyes and avoid the kind of failures David had. (For instance, for the first one, you might glean the general principle "Know God so well that I trust Him in challenging times.") Then write some ways you can put this into practice (e.g., "Get to know God better by reading a portion of Scripture and recording in a journal what I discover about God.")

Never doubt that God is with you!

David's Pattern	General Principle for My Life	Ways I Can Practice This Principle
David knew God.		
David did not fight Goliath for fame or riches for himself.		
David didn't depend on man-made weapons or strategies.		

Choose one small action to do this week.

Create a Project

1. One reason God still saw David as "a man after His own heart" even after David's many failures was that when David was confronted with his sin, he repented. Read Psalm 51, a prayer David wrote after Nathan pointed out his sin with Bathsheba. Then try one of the following projects to practice the spiritual discipline of confession.

Create in me a clean heart, O God.

Psalm 51:10

a. Using Psalm 51 as a guide, write your own prayer of repentance. Put the psalm into your own words.

b. Spend a few moments asking the Holy Spirit to point out where your thoughts, words, or actions have failed to follow His ways. Write each failure in one of the spaces in the picture on the facing page. When you have finished, find some brightly colored markers or colored pencils and color over the words. As you color, confess each sin and thank God that He will "blot out all [your] iniquities" (Psalm 51:9).

2. Listen to songs about confession and God's forgiveness. Try "Forgiven" by Sanctus Real or "Psalm 51 Song" by Jason Silver. Or sing hymns like "Come, Thou Fount of Every Blessing" (*LSB* 686) or "Create in Me" (*LSB* 956).

Chapter 4

Jeremiah: Poorly Received Prophet

REFLECT ON THE READING

1. Do you equate success with popularity? Where do you see this tendency in modern culture?

2. When has God called you to a role you felt unqualified for but found that God equipped you for the work?

3. In this chapter, we learned that God doesn't measure success in the number of trophies or the size of your audience. He uses the measuring tape of faithfulness. How do you see this in Jeremiah's life? How does this truth encourage you in your own life?

4. What is your biggest takeaway from this chapter?

DIG INTO THE WORD

Jeremiah's story takes place in the fifty-two chapters of the book bearing his name. You may want to read the whole account of his life, but right now we will focus on one of Jeremiah's most difficult times. Read Jeremiah 37–38. Then answer these questions about the four important elements of a biblical narrative.

1. **Repeated words and phrases.** a. Complete this chart by finding these important phrases repeated in these chapters.

PHRASE	VERSES WHERE THIS PHRASE IS FOUND
"The word of the LORD"	
"Thus says the LORD"	

    b. Why are these phrases especially significant for Jeremiah's story?

2. **Actions.** In these chapters, another character plays a major role in Jeremiah's life—King Zedekiah. Look at the following verses and write what the king did. Then make a generalization about his character. I have done the first one for you.

VERSE	ACTION	WHAT THE ACTION REVEALS ABOUT ZEDEKIAH'S CHARACTER
Jeremiah 37:16–17	Zedekiah secretly sent for Jeremiah to come and talk with him.	Zedekiah wanted a word from the Lord but he didn't want anyone else to know about it. He was secretive.
Jeremiah 37:18–21		
Jeremiah 38:4–6		
Jeremiah 38:8–10		

3. **Dialogue.** a. Now look at Jeremiah's words in chapters 37 and 38. Write what he said and what his words demonstrate about his character. I've done the first one for you.

Verse	Jeremiah's Words	What His Words Reveal about His Character
Jeremiah 37:6–10	Jeremiah told the king that the Babylonians would return and capture Jerusalem.	Jeremiah obediently shared God's word, even when he knew the message wouldn't be popular.
Jeremiah 37:17		
Jeremiah 38:1–4		

b. Jeremiah and Zedekiah couldn't have been more different. Review what you just learned and compare and contrast the two men.

4. **Narration.** Now look at the narration of the story (everything but the dialogue). What happens to Jeremiah in these chapters?

a. Jeremiah 37:11–16

b. Jeremiah 37:21

c. Jeremiah 38:6

d. Jeremiah 38:10–13

e. What did you learn about Jeremiah's character after reading about all that happened to him?

APPLY THE WORD TO YOUR LIFE

Read Jeremiah 1, which describes how God called this Old Testament prophet.

1. Look at verse 5. The word *knew* signifies more than recognizing someone; it indicates a relationship with someone. Also, the word *consecrated* means God set apart Jeremiah for a particular purpose. Now read the verse as if God were speaking it directly to you. What does it mean to you that God "knew you" and "consecrated you" for a specific purpose even before you were born?

2. Look at verses 7 and 8 and personalize them with words that express *your* feelings.

   a. Jeremiah didn't see himself as an orator. Where do you feel unqualified? Fill in the blank: I am only _____. (For instance, when I began speaking to women's groups, I didn't see myself as a speaker. I would have said, "I'm only a pastor's wife, not a pastor or speaker.")

   b. What do you feel God is calling you to do? Fill in the blank: Whatever I command you, you shall _____. (For instance, when I felt God calling me to give presentations to women's groups, I felt God saying, "Whatever I command you, you shall speak.")

   c. How does this calling make you anxious? Fill in the blank: Do not be afraid of _____.

d. The last sentence of Jeremiah 1:8 says, "I am with you to deliver you, declares the LORD." How does this chase away your fears?

3. Look at Jeremiah 1:9–10. After God called Jeremiah to speak for Him, He touched Jeremiah's mouth and said, "Behold, I have put My words in your mouth" (v. 9). How has God equipped you for your calling?

4. Reread verses 18 and 19. God promised to make Jeremiah "an iron pillar" because the government officials, priests, and people would all fight against him. However, God follows up the bad news with some good news.

a. What does God promise at the end of verse 19?

b. How can this encourage you when your work for the Lord doesn't have the kind of success you envisioned?

CREATE A PROJECT

1. God told Jeremiah to go to the potter's house (Jeremiah 18) and watch the potter. There God told Jeremiah that the clay in the hands of the potter was like Israel in the hands of God. The apostle Paul also uses a pottery analogy in Romans 9:20: "But who are you, O man, to answer back to God? Will what is molded say to its molder, 'Why have you made me like this?'"

Consider making a simple clay pot, shaping it from a fist-size lump of air-drying modeling compound. While you are molding it, ask God to mold you according to His purpose. Etch a decorative design on the outside as desired using a skewer or other pointed object. Detailed instructions can be found on the internet.

2. On several occasions, Jeremiah poured out his heart to God, honestly telling Him, "I do not know how to speak" (Jeremiah 1:6), or asking, "Why is my pain unceasing, my wound incurable?" (Jeremiah 15:18). God hears our cries and then offers His comfort and strength.

   One of my favorite spiritual disciplines, "Palms Down, Palms Up Prayer," gives the space to pour out our concerns to God and then receive from Him what we need.

   a. Read Jeremiah 15:15–21.

   b. Sit in a comfortable chair in a quiet place. Place your hands on your legs palms down to symbolize your desire to release your concerns to God. Like Jeremiah, pour out your pain, your anxieties, your feelings.

   c. Then turn your hands palms up to symbolize your desire to receive from God. Meditate on the words God spoke to Jeremiah, and ask God to also give you what you need in this moment.

3. Sing hymns about God's call on our lives: "How Clear Is Our Vocation, Lord" (*LSB* 853) or "Take My Life and Let It Be (*LSB* 783, 784). Or listen to "Write Your Story" by Francesca Battistelli or "The Potter's Hand" by Hillsong Worship.

CHAPTER 5

JOHN THE BAPTIST: PECULIAR PREACHER

REFLECT ON THE READING

1. If you heard about a strange man who wore camel's-hair clothing and ate bugs, would you journey into the wilderness to see him? Why or why not?

2. How did John's lifestyle fit his message? What does your lifestyle say about what you stand for?

3. In this chapter, we read, "When we live to glorify Jesus, we don't mind becoming the warm-up band or the backup singers." Do you agree with this statement? How have you seen this in your own life or the lives of people you know?

4. What is your biggest takeaway from this chapter?

DIG INTO THE WORD

John the Baptist's story is found in various places in the Gospels: Matthew 3, 11, 14, and 17; Mark 1 and 6; Luke 1, 3, and 7; and John 1 and 3. We will dig into Matthew 3 because it presents John the Baptist's early ministry and his encounter with Jesus.

1. **Repeated words and phrases.** a. Read Matthew 3 and complete this chart by finding these important words repeated in this chapter.

WORD	VERSES WHERE THIS WORD IS FOUND
repent, repentance	
baptize, Baptism	

      b. Why are these key words for the life of John the Baptist?

2. **Actions.** Read through Matthew 3 again and focus on the specific verses listed below. Write down any significant actions that John the Baptist performed. Then write what the action reveals about his character.

VERSE	ACTION	WHAT THE ACTION REVEALS ABOUT JOHN THE BAPTIST'S CHARACTER
Matthew 3:1		
Matthew 3:4		
Matthew 3:6		

3. **Dialogue.** Now look at what John the Baptist says in Matthew 3. Summarize who he spoke to, what he said, and what his words reveal about his character.

Verse	Who John the Baptist Spoke To	What He Said	What His Words Reveal about His Character
Matthew 3:7–10			
Matthew 3:11–12			
Matthew 3:14			

4. **Narration.** Look at what the narrator describes in the following passages. Write what happened and how these events might have affected John the Baptist.

   a. Matthew 3:5–6

   b. Matthew 3:16–17

5. After focusing on the repeated words, actions, dialogue, and narration, what did you learn about John the Baptist that you didn't know before?

APPLY THE WORD TO YOUR LIFE

Read John 3:22–30.

1. How would you describe the attitude of John the Baptist's disciples? What do they seem worried about?

2. Does John have the same concerns? How can you tell?

3. John the Baptist said, "A person cannot receive even one thing unless it is given him from heaven" (John 3:27).

    a. Put his statement into your own words.

    b. What ministries has God given you right now? (Don't limit ministries to church work. Think also about your roles at work, at home, and in your community.)

4. John the Baptist compared himself to the friend of the bridegroom (John 3:29).

    a. Think of when you have been part of a wedding party or attended a wedding and observed the attendants. Describe the role of bridesmaid or groomsman.

    b. How does this illustration help you understand your role in the Christian life?

5. John the Baptist's famous line "He must increase, but I must decrease" (John 3:30) is not easy to live out.

    a. Why do we humans find this difficult?

    b. Looking at the list of ministries you wrote in response to question 3b, what are some specific ways you can become less while helping Jesus appear greater to those around you?

CREATE A PROJECT

1. John the Baptist made a name for himself by baptizing people who had confessed their sins. Acknowledging their failures and shortcomings made them aware of their need for a Savior and prepared them for the coming of the Messiah.

Whenever you wash your face,
Remember your baptism.

MARTIN LUTHER

Gracious Father, thank You for the gift of Baptism, which Your Son has established by His Word and Promise. Teach us to treasure all that Jesus has done for us in His cross and resurrection. Give us confidence that through our Baptism we bear Your holy name and so are Your holy children for time and eternity, through the same Jesus Christ, our Lord.
Amen.

However, John the Baptist understood the difference between his Baptism and the Baptism Christ would bring. He said, "I baptize you with water for repentance, but He who is coming after me is mightier than I, whose sandals I am not worthy to carry. He will baptize you with the Holy Spirit and fire" (Matthew 3:11). So now, as New Testament believers, when we are baptized in the name of the triune God, we receive more than a sign of our repentance; we receive a Baptism that "works forgiveness of sins, rescues from death and the devil, and gives eternal salvation to all who believe this."[99]

Tradition holds that Martin Luther taught, "Whenever you wash your face, remember your Baptism." Let's make this a practice this week. Make a copy of the sign on the facing page (or make your own sign) and tape it to your bathroom mirror. Then, every time you wash your face this week, repeat the prayer, rejoicing that God has washed away all of your sins and shortcomings. What a gift it is to know that whenever we have failed, whenever we've made a mess of our lives, we have forgiveness because of Christ's death and resurrection.[100]

2. Sing or listen to music that reinforces what we've learned: "On Jordan's Bank the Baptist's Cry" (*LSB* 344), "Not unto Us" (*LSB* 558), "More of You" by Colton Dixon, or "Grace Like Rain" by Todd Agnew.

CHAPTER 6

THE SAMARITAN WOMAN: FIVE-TIME FAILURE

REFLECT ON THE READING

1. In this world, who is "most likely to succeed"? What qualities or privileges help a person rise to the top?

2. If the villagers of Sychar had taken a vote, they might have given the woman at the well the distinction of "the least likely to succeed." Why might that be true? What strikes did she have against her?

3. Why do you think Jesus chose to reveal Himself to this unlikely woman?

4. What is your biggest takeaway from this chapter?

DIG INTO THE WORD

We find the story of the Samaritan woman in John 4:1–42. Read these verses and then answer these questions about the four important elements of a biblical narrative.

1. **Repeated words and phrases.** a. What words are repeated often in this passage? Complete this chart by adding more words that appear often and then writing the verses where these words are found in John 4:1–42.

Word	Verses Where This Word Is Found
thirst, thirsty	

b. Why are these words important in the Samaritan woman's story?

c. What temporary things have you used to try to satisfy your spiritual thirst?

2. **Actions.** In this short account that contains mostly dialogue, we don't see a lot of action. But the Samaritan woman does two significant things. In the chart below, record her actions and what they reveal about her character.

Verse	Action	What the Action Reveals about the Samaritan Woman's Character
John 4:6–7		
John 4:28		

3. **Dialogue.** John 4 contains a lot of dialogue. Let's look at two important verses where the Samaritan woman speaks.

   a. We have learned that the first time a person speaks in Scripture often reveals something about his or her character. The Samaritan woman's first words are recorded in John 4:9. Read this verse and write what her words reveal about how she sees herself.

   b. Now look at her last words in chapter 4. Read John 4:29. What do you think these words reveal about her character and how the encounter with Jesus changed her?

4. **Narration.** Although this chapter contains very little narration, the description we find there reveals a lot about the success of the woman at the well. Read the following passages and write what you learn about the effect of the Samaritan woman's testimony.

   a. John 4:30

   b. John 4:39–42

5. After focusing on the repeated words, actions, dialogue, and narration, what did you learn about the Samaritan woman that you didn't know before?

APPLY THE WORD TO YOUR LIFE

Read John 4:16–26.

1. Jesus revealed the woman's past. What did He reveal?

2. Looking closely at this passage, how would you describe Jesus' attitude toward the woman?

3. Jesus knows everything about your past too. Does this make you uncomfortable? Does Jesus' interaction with the woman at the well comfort you? How?

4. When Jesus talked about her many husbands, the woman changed the subject and talked about the controversy the Jews and Samaritans had about the proper place to worship. Do you think she changed the subject to avoid talking about her failures, or because she felt the need to confess and worship God? Explain your answer.

5. When the Holy Spirit confronts you with your sin, what is your first reaction? Do you avoid the topic as much as possible? Or do you confess and feel the relief of forgiveness? Do you think the story of the Samaritan woman changes your response?

6. The Samaritan woman recognized that the stranger she was speaking to might be the Messiah. This filled her with such excitement that she left her water jug behind and ran to tell her neighbors. How has the Good News of the Messiah changed your life?

CREATE A PROJECT

1. We saw in the story of the Samaritan woman that we don't need a degree in theology or a pristine past to have success in God's kingdom. Even though the Samaritan woman had many strikes against her, many people believed in Jesus because of her testimony. Let's begin to follow her example by making a Bible bookmark that will remind us to pray for the people in our lives who need to know the Messiah.

   a. Photocopy the image below and cut out the bookmark.

   b. On the back of the bookmark, write the names of family members, co-workers, and neighbors who don't yet believe in Jesus.

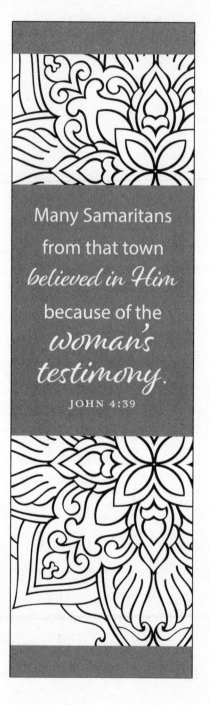

Many Samaritans from that town *believed in Him* because of the *woman's testimony.*

JOHN 4:39

c. Use markers or colored pencils to color the shapes on the front of the bookmark. While coloring, pray for the people you listed on the back. Pray that God will make you an effective witness of His grace.

d. Keep the bookmark in your Bible or study book and continue to pray that these people would thirst to know the Messiah!

2. The woman at the well told the people of Sychar, "Come, see a man who told me all that I ever did. Can this be the Christ?" (John 4:29). She simply told of her encounter with Jesus—that's exactly what a witness does. We can also practice the spiritual discipline of witness by telling others about our encounters with Jesus. You don't need a twelve-point evangelism outline to be an effective witness, but it can help to think about your faith story. Grab a sheet of paper and write about your relationship with the Messiah by using these questions as prompts:

How has knowing Jesus changed you?

How does knowing Jesus fulfill your desires and quench your spiritual thirst?

How would your life be different if you didn't know Jesus?

What events in your life have confirmed your faith in a loving and omnipotent God?

Now, when the Holy Spirit prompts you to tell someone else about Jesus, you can combine your story with God's Word to share the Gospel.

3. To help internalize some of the lessons you learned in this chapter, listen to and/or sing songs like "My Jesus" by Anne Wilson, "The Well" by Casting Crowns, "I Heard the Voice of Jesus Say" (*LSB* 699), and "Hark, the Voice of Jesus Calling" (*LSB* 827).

CHAPTER 7

PETER: DYNAMIC DENIER

REFLECT ON THE READING

1. What is your favorite story about Peter? How do you relate to that story?

2. We often define success in terms of "better" and "best." How does Peter's experience with Jesus show us that God does not view success as being better than someone else?

3. Write your reaction to this quote from the reading: "Because of Peter's story, we find confidence in the truth that when we have failed, we can still run . . . to Jesus, the source of mercy and grace."

4. What is your biggest takeaway from this chapter?

DIG INTO THE WORD

We find Peter's story throughout the Gospels and in the first fifteen chapters of the Book of Acts. Peter also wrote two general epistles: 1 and 2 Peter. Here we will examine a couple of passages from the Gospels.

1. **Repeated words and phrases.** a. Read Matthew 26:69–75 and complete this chart by finding important words repeated in these verses.

Verses	Key Word Found in These Verses
Matthew 26:70, 72, 75	*denied*
Matthew 26:70, 72, 74	*I don't know the man*

b. Why are these key words for the life of Peter?

2. **Actions.** This time, we will take a look at Peter's actions by examining the story of his denial in all four Gospels. Begin with Mark's account and write down the actions you see Peter take. Then read the other Gospel passages and take note of any differences you see from Mark's account.

Gospel	Mark 14:66–72	Matthew 26:69–75	Luke 22:54–62	John 18:15–18, 25–27
Peter's Actions				

3. **Dialogue.** a. During Peter's time in the courtyard of the home of the high priest, he says "I don't know" three times, but his words change a little each time. Read Matthew 26:69–75 one more time and observe how Peter's denials escalate. I did the first one for you.

Verse	What Peter Said	How His Words Escalated
Matthew 26:70	"I don't know what you mean."	At first, Peter only said he didn't know what the servant girl meant. He didn't say that he didn't know Jesus.
Matthew 26:72		
Matthew 26:74		

b. The Greek word for "know" in this passage is *eidō*, which can mean simply "to have knowledge of or to see and recognize." How well did Peter know Jesus in this sense?

c. Another meaning of *eidō* is "to have regard for one, cherish, pay attention to."[101] How well did Peter know Jesus in this sense? And how might his misunderstanding of the role of the Messiah have affected his knowing?

4. **Narration.** Luke included an important detail in his narration that the other Gospel writers omitted. Read Luke 22:61–62.

a. What is the important detail Luke includes?

b. How does this change the story for you? How do you think it changed Peter?

APPLY THE WORD TO YOUR LIFE

1. I find it very comforting that Jesus specifically prayed for Peter, knowing the great temptation he would face. Jesus said, "Simon, Simon, behold, Satan demanded to have you, that he might sift you like wheat, but I have prayed for you that your faith may not fail. And when you have turned again, strengthen your brothers" (Luke 22:31–32).

    a. According to this passage, why did Jesus pray for Peter?

    b. What did He pray for Peter?

    c. Romans 8:34 says, "Christ Jesus is the one who died— more than that, who was raised—who is at the right hand of God, who indeed is interceding for us." How does it comfort you that Jesus also prays for you?

2. Jesus not only prayed for Peter, but He also instructed Peter to pray for himself. Jesus said, "Watch and pray that you may not enter into temptation. The spirit indeed is willing, but the flesh is weak" (Mark 14:38).

    a. What was Peter to pray for?

b. Why did Peter need to pray this prayer?

c. Jesus instructed all of His followers to pray "And lead us not into temptation" (Matthew 6:13) in the Lord's Prayer. Take an honest look at your prayer life. How often do you mindfully pray this prayer? How can the story of Peter help you to be more proactive in watching and praying?

CREATE A PROJECT

1. One of my favorite spiritual practices is meditating on Bible stories. In my Bible study *Soul Spa*, I gave some guidance on this practice: "Read a Gospel story and ask the Spirit to guide your thoughts. See the scene in your mind. What sounds do you hear? What scents are in the air? Use all five senses to put you there."[102] Take time today to read the story of Jesus and Peter's conversation after the Lord's resurrection in John 21:15–23 and visualize the setting. As you read, put yourself in Peter's place. What feelings does this stir up? How does it shape your view of Jesus? How does it affect your view of yourself? Write your reactions below.

2. Use the gift of music to remind yourself of all you've learned. Sing "Go to Dark Gethsemane" (*LSB* 436) or "Were You There" (*LSB* 456). Or listen to "Call It Grace" by Unspoken, "Mended" by Matthew West, or "Graves into Gardens" by Elevation Worship.

CHAPTER 8

PAUL: POWERFUL PERSECUTOR

REFLECT ON THE READING

1. Think back to a time when you ran a race or watched a race. How were the winners treated? the losers? How does that compare to the race of real life?

2. What is your reaction to the story of Team Hoyt? Would you say you are running the race of everyday life trying to be in the position of Dick—running in your own power—or in the position of Rick—being propelled by the Father? Explain your answer.

3. In this chapter, we read, "Can we come to the point where we, like Paul, rejoice in weakness, in seeming failure, simply because it means an opportunity to rely even more on the grace of God?" What might rejoicing in weakness look like in your life right now?

4. What is your biggest takeaway from this chapter?

DIG INTO THE WORD

We can read about Paul in the Book of Acts and the thirteen epistles he wrote. Here we will dig into Acts 9, where Jesus meets Saul on the road to Damascus. Read Acts 9:1–25 and examine the narrative.

1. **Repeated words and phrases.** a. Record any words or phrases you see repeated in this passage and the verses where these words appear. In this passage, you might include related words. For instance, there are many words related to sight: "see," "saw," "sight," "vision." You could put all of these in the first box and record where these words are found.

Word or Phrase	Verses Where These Appear

b. Looking at these repeated words and phrases, summarize some of the themes of this passage.

c. Why are these themes important in Paul's life?

2. **Actions.** Now look at Saul's actions in this passage. Write what he did at various points of the story and what his actions demonstrate about his character.

Verses	Action	What the Action Reveals about Saul's Character
Before meeting Jesus Acts 9:1–2	*Looked for Christians*	*He wasn't a Christian*
After meeting Jesus but before regaining his sight Acts 9:3–17	*He saw Jesus + Lost his sight But Believed*	*He Became a Christian*
After regaining his sight Acts 9:18–25		*A Believer*

3. **Dialogue.** Remember that the first time a person speaks in Scripture or even in a certain scene often reveals something about his or her character.

   a. The first recorded words of Saul/Paul are found in Acts 9:5. What does he say there?

   Who are You LORD.

   b. What does this reveal about his character?

   He Knew who the Lord was

4. **Narration.** Now look at the narration of the story (everything but the dialogue). What does the biblical narrator reveal about the character of the following people?

   a. Paul

   b. Ananias

   c. Damascus disciples

   d. Jews in Damascus

APPLY THE WORD TO YOUR LIFE

Let's find ways we can live out the principles of success we learned from Paul's life. Look at each principle, read the corresponding Bible passage, then answer the questions for each.

1. **Striving for worldly success can be a detriment to our spiritual success.** Read Philippians 3:4–7. How will this principle change how you view a failure or disappointment in your life? How will it affect what you do when God does grant success?

2. **Success is knowing Christ.** Read Philippians 3:8–11. If you lived with that definition of success, how would it modify your life goals? your five-year plans? your daily to-do lists?

3. **Success is not perfection but transformation.** Read Philippians 3:12–14. Look back at the past year of your life and list ways the Holy Spirit has transformed you. Then write a prayer asking Jesus to help you continually press on for the success of God's grace in your heart, even as you are covered with the perfect righteousness of Christ.

CREATE A PROJECT

1. Take a personal spiritual retreat.

> After Paul met Jesus on the road to Damascus, he spent about ten years in seclusion and anonymity in Arabia and Tarsus. God had specifically called Paul to carry His name to the Gentiles (Acts 9:15), but Paul didn't immediately begin this ministry. The Lord often calls His people to times of solitude to give them time to know Him in a deeper way and to form their character. Remember that God doesn't define success by what we accomplish but by how well we know Him.
>
> While God doesn't call most of us to ten years of seclusion, He did call His disciples to "Come away by yourselves to a desolate place and rest a while" (Mark 6:31). A personal spiritual retreat can help us pull away from the hustle of this world and quiet our souls enough to hear God's voice. I try to block out one morning each month to take a break with God. To sit quietly in His presence. To sink deep into His Word.
>
> You might be asking, "What do you do at a personal spiritual retreat?" Here's my process:
>
> > I read God's Word and journal what I hear God speaking to me. I might use the passage for the day from my Bible-reading plan or ask God for a specific passage to meditate on.
> >
> > I pour out my struggles, worries, and disappointments, asking God to make sense out of everything.

I get out my schedule and to-do list and pray for God to give me His perspective and His priorities.

I spend time resting in God's love for me.

For more ideas, you can find a free resource on my website: http://www.sharlafritz.com/2016/05/7-habits-promote-soul -rest-personal-retreat/

You might not have time for a retreat today, but right now look at your calendar and schedule one. Fill out the following form to commit to a personal spiritual retreat in the near future.

When I will take a spiritual retreat

_____

Where I will take this retreat (at a nearby park? hotel? retreat center?)

_____

What I will take on this retreat (Bible? journal? devotional?)

_____

2. Use music to draw your heart closer to Jesus. Perhaps use these songs on your personal spiritual retreat (or during a coffee break today!). Try "Strong Enough" by Matthew West or "You Are My All in All" by Dennis Jernigan. Sing "Chief of Sinners Though I Be" (*LSB* 611) or "Rock of Ages, Cleft for Me" (*LSB* 761).

Closing Activity

To review all you've learned in this study, fill out this simple chart. Look back in the study. Which Scriptures encouraged your heart? What did you learn that can help you embrace God's measure of success rather than live by the world's standard? To identify key lessons, you might review the "When You Feel . . ." section of each chapter, where we examined truths about success and failure. Or you might look at how you answered the question "What is your biggest takeaway from this chapter?" in the Study Guide.

Biblical Character	Scripture That Encouraged Me	Key Lesson I Learned
1. Joseph		
2. Rahab		
3. David		
4. Jeremiah		

5. John the Baptist		
6. The Samaritan Woman		
7. Peter		
8. Paul		

Next, consider how this study has impacted your life by answering these questions:

1. To which of the biblical characters did you most strongly relate?

2. How have you changed through this study?

3. What lesson about success and failure do you want to carry with you as you move through life?

Parting Thoughts

We live in a success-worshiping society. Athletes and pop stars live for the roar of the crowd. Actors inhabit the spotlight and thrive on applause. Businessmen and -women strive for upward mobility in their professions.

But God does not view success the same way the world does. He doesn't reserve places in heaven only for those who earn six figures or write best sellers. The Lord grants each of us the greatest success of all—salvation—as a free gift. Eternal life comes only through the work of Jesus on the cross and not through our own achievements.

Here is God's wonderful and free plan of salvation in His Word:

"For all have sinned and fall short of the glory of God" (Romans 3:23). No one is perfect. Everyone fails to meet God's standard of sinlessness. This sin prevents us from coming to Him and from entering heaven.

"For God so loved the world, that He gave His only Son, that whoever believes in Him should not perish but have eternal life" (John 3:16). God loved us so much that He sent His own Son to take the punishment we deserve for our sins and mistakes. Jesus' death enables us to live with God—forever.

"For by grace you have been saved through faith. And this is not your own doing; it is the gift of God" (Ephesians 2:8). God gives us faith to believe in Jesus. His grace and mercy save us from death.

"But to all who did receive Him, who believed in His name, He gave the right to become children of God" (John 1:12). By receiving Jesus in the waters of Baptism and the holy Word of God, we become part of God's family.

I invite you to pray this prayer to the God who loves you and calls you to be part of His family:

> Father in heaven, I realize that I am a sinner and fall short of
> what You want for my life. I know that I cannot save myself

or earn eternal life. Thank You for sending Your Son, Jesus, to die for me. Through the power of His resurrection, You have made me alive eternally. Help me to turn from my sins and follow You. Thank You that although I may still fail, You will forgive me because Jesus paid the price for my sins. Thank You for Your gift of faith in Jesus, my Savior, and for the promise of eternal life with You. In Jesus' name I pray. Amen.

God speaks His words of grace to you. Through God's free gift of faith in Jesus, you now are part of God's family!

Acknowledgments

Success as an author is often measured in numbers of books sold, but only God sees the true success that happens in numbers of lives transformed. I pray that the Holy Spirit will continue to change lives as He changed mine through the writing of this book.

This book could not be a success without the following! I wish to thank

God: Thank You for including the stories of failures and misfits in Your Word. Writing this book has helped me learn Your definition of success.

John: Thank you for reading and rereading my words and for sharing your own story of God's successful work in your ministry.

Family: To Mom, Anna and Nate, Nathaniel and Mary, thank you all for your love, prayers, and support.

To writing friends: Afton Rorvik, thank you not only for your excellent writing advice but for your friendship. You balance the long hours at the computer with your inspiration and support. To Jan May, thanks for lunches and brunches, encouragement and laughter.

To those who lent their stories to the book: Thank you John, Pastor Ken Baisden, and Mariaisabel Morales. Your examples of God-given success inspire us all.

To Concordia Publishing House: Thanks to all who work so hard to edit, design, and market books that nurture faith in God. A special shout-out goes to Peggy Kuethe, editor and friend, who always makes my writing more successful than it would be without her!

STUDY GUIDE ANSWERS

CHAPTER 1

Reflect on the Reading: Answers will vary. **Dig into the Word:** (1.) Answers will vary but might include the following:

WORD OR PHRASE	VERSES WHERE THESE APPEAR
"The LORD was with Joseph."	Genesis 39:2, 3, 21
successful/succeed	vv. 2, 3, 23
found favor	vv. 4, 21
blessed/blessing	2 times in v. 5
in Joseph's charge	vv. 6, 8, 22
no concern	vv. 6, 8, 23
"Lie with me."	vv. 7, 12, 14

Possible answers for themes of the chapter: Success comes from God. God grants favor. God will always be with us, even in our darkest times. Shun temptation. (2a.) Joseph repeatedly worked hard and earned the respect of his overseers. Joseph repeatedly earned positions of management. Joseph repeatedly refused the advances of Potiphar's wife. (2b.) Some aspects of Joseph's character: hardworking, good at managing people and resources, moral and God-fearing. (3a.) The first time Joseph speaks in Genesis 39 is verse 8, where he says, "Behold, because of me my master has no concern about anything in the house, and he has put everything that he has in my charge. He is not greater in this house than I am, nor has he kept back anything from me except you, because you are his wife. How then can I do this great wickedness and sin against God?" (3b.) Joseph's words reveal that he is trustworthy and faithful to his master and to God. (4a.) It seems obvious that Potiphar liked Joseph. He put Joseph in charge because Joseph brought him success. He noticed that Yahweh was with Joseph, so perhaps he even became a believer. (4b.) Potiphar's wife had feelings of lust for handsome Joseph. She was seductive, unfaithful in her marriage, and untruthful. She seems extremely self-centered. (4c.) The jailer seems lazy. Ordinarily, it would not have been wise to put one inmate in charge of the others, but it seems his motive for doing so was Joseph's ability to succeed in whatever he did. (4d.) The Bible doesn't spell out Joseph's feelings, and we wonder how he sensed God's presence and love. But the text does tell us Joseph shunned his mistress's advances because he respected his master and honored God's Law. The narrator helps us understand the providence of God by continually declaring that God was with Joseph, even when circumstances would have made people doubt that. The narrator tells us over and over that Joseph was successful even when he was in "unsuccessful" positions, thus showing that God's view of success doesn't necessarily look like importance. The narrator tells us, "The LORD caused all that he did to succeed" (v. 3), emphasizing the fact that it is God who grants success. **Apply the Word to Your Life:** Answers will vary. **Create a Project:** (1.) Answers will vary. Possible answers for *S*: satisfied with God's plan, strong in God, small in the world's eyes, spotless in God's eyes. Possible answers for *U*: unassuming, unshrinking, unique, unselfish, untarnished, useful. Possible answers for *C*: caring, calling on the Lord, cheering others on, certain of God's presence, contributing to a common goal, confident in God. Possible answers for *E*: empowered by God, encouraging to others, extraordinary in God's eyes, exemplary. (2.) Answers will vary. (3.) Music.

CHAPTER 2

Reflect on the Reading: Answers will vary. **Dig into the Word:** (1a.) Answers will vary but might include the following:

WORD OR PHRASE	VERSES WHERE THESE APPEAR
"the LORD"	Joshua 2:9, 10, 11, 12, 14
pursue/pursuers	vv. 7, 16, 22
fear/no spirit	vv. 9, 11
melt	vv. 9, 11, 24
heard	vv. 10, 11
guiltless	vv. 17, 19, 20
scarlet cord	vv. 18, 21

(1b.) Themes might include the following: Yahweh is the one true God. The fear of the citizens of Jericho. Hearing about God is the first step toward faith. "Guiltless" is used by the Israelite spies in terms of their obligations to Rahab and their lack of guilt if she doesn't keep her end of the bargain, but "guiltless" becomes an important theme as God forgives Rahab and makes her one of His own. (2.) Some of Rahab's actions that display her faith include the following: She puts her own life in danger to protect the men representing Yahweh. She takes the side of God and the Israelites instead of the side of her own people. (3a.) Rahab's first speech reveals her quick thinking and her bravery. (3b.) Rahab's words in Joshua 2:8–13 demonstrate that she has faith in the one true God and that she is concerned about her family. They also show she is savvy—she knows enough about the ways of the king's men to instruct the Israelite spies to hide in the hills for three days before going back across the Jordan. (3c.) Rahab does lie, which is against God's commands. But telling falsehoods in war to protect what is right is accepted practice. She lies to protect the Israelite men and the cause of almighty God. (4a.) The Israelite spies were brave and obedient enough to follow Joshua's orders (Joshua 2:1). They respected Rahab enough to follow her advice to flee into the hills for three days (vv. 22–23). They were faithful to their word, going back to save Rahab and her family (Joshua 6:23). (4b.) The people of Jericho were afraid. They had lost their courage (Joshua 2:9; 6:1). (4c.) Joshua was obedient to the Lord's instructions. He also demonstrated faith because these instructions did not follow the usual procedure for defeating a city (Joshua 6:8–11). He was an effective leader because God was with him (Joshua 6:26–27). (4d.) Rahab was quick-thinking, hiding the spies under the flax stalks (Joshua 2:6). **Apply the Word to Your Life:** (1a.) Four times. (1b.) To emphasize God's saving grace and that our success does not depend on our goodness. (2.) Answers will vary. (3.) Answers will vary. (4.) Answers will vary. **Create a Project:** (1.) Bookmark. (2.) Worship. (3.) Music.

CHAPTER 3

Reflect on the Reading: Answers will vary. **Dig into the Word:** (1a.)

VERSE	DESCRIPTION OF DAVID
1 Samuel 17:14	"David was the youngest."
1 Samuel 17:33	"You are but a youth."
1 Samuel 17:42	"He was but a youth, ruddy and handsome in appearance."
1 Samuel 17:55	"Youth."

(1b.) "Youth" or "young" is repeated, probably to emphasize that David was unqualified to win over Goliath. God's power defeated the giant. (2.)

VERSE	ACTION	WHAT THE ACTION REVEALS ABOUT DAVID'S CHARACTER
1 Samuel 17:15	David went back and forth from playing the harp for King Saul to tending the sheep.	Even after having "royal duties," David didn't consider himself too important to do the humble work of tending the sheep.
1 Samuel 17:17–20	David took provisions to his brothers.	He demonstrated obedience to his father.
1 Samuel 17:38–39	David tried on the armor but took it off.	He did not rely on man-made protection. He trusted in God.
1 Samuel 17:40	David took his staff and five smooth stones and approached the Philistine.	David was confident because he trusted in God.
1 Samuel 17:48–51	He ran quickly and struck Goliath with a stone.	He didn't hesitate; he had faith in God's strength and protection.

(3a.)

Verse	Who David Spoke To	What David's Words Reveal about His Character
1 Samuel 17:26	The Israelite soldiers	He was concerned about God's honor.
1 Samuel 17:29	His eldest brother	He defended his innocence and wanted his brothers to see that they should be fighting Goliath instead of him.
1 Samuel 17:32–37	Saul	He had confidence in God because God had saved him from danger before.
1 Samuel 17:45–47	Goliath	David knew that with God as his secret weapon, he could defeat Goliath. He fought to demonstrate the power of the God of Israel.

(3b.) David's words reveal a deep trust in God's strength and protection. He sees his mission as demonstrating to the world that the God of Israel is the true God and cannot be defeated. (3c.) Most of the time, David did depend on God's power and strength. But when he abandoned trust in God's power and laws, he experienced defeat and failure. (4a.) Goliath's size and armor are described in detail. His confidence was based on those things. (4b.) The Israelite soldiers were afraid of Goliath. They compared their own size and might with the giant's instead of comparing God's power with Goliath's. (4c.) Saul allowed a boy to go out to battle instead of taking on the giant himself, even though Saul is described as being a head taller than the other men of Israel. He did not have the same faith David did. **Apply the Word to Your Life:** Answers will vary, but might include the following:

David's Pattern	General Principle for My Life	Ways I Can Practice This Principle
David knew God.	Know God so well that I trust Him in challenging times.	Get to know God better by reading a portion of Scripture and recording in a journal what I discover about God.
David did not fight Goliath for fame or riches for himself.	Don't work for my own success, but work to give God glory.	Before I start my tasks for the day, ask God to help me work for Him.
David didn't depend on man-made weapons or strategies.	Don't depend on self-help books or experts. Research ways to solve problems, but pray for God's wisdom.	Make a sign reading "For the battle is the LORD's" (1 Samuel 17:47) to remind me that God's got my back.

Create a Project: (1.) Answers will vary. (2.) Music.

CHAPTER 4

Reflect on the Reading: Answers will vary. **Dig into the Word:** (1a.)

Phrase	Verses Where This Phrase Is Found
"The word of the LORD"	Jeremiah 37:2, 6, 17
"Thus says the LORD"	Jeremiah 37:7, 9; 38:2, 3, 17

(1b.) From the very beginning, God declared to Jeremiah, "I have put My words in your mouth" (Jeremiah 1:9). The prophet faithfully spoke what God told him to say even though the message was often unpopular.

(2.)

VERSE	ACTION	WHAT THE ACTION REVEALS ABOUT ZEDEKIAH'S CHARACTER
Jeremiah 37:16–17	Zedekiah secretly sent for Jeremiah to come and talk with him.	Zedekiah wanted a word from the Lord but he didn't want anyone else to know about it. He was secretive.
Jeremiah 37:18–21	Zedekiah granted Jeremiah's request to be released from the dungeon.	He could be merciful.
Jeremiah 38:4–6	Zedekiah listened to the officials and allowed them to do whatever they wanted to the prophet.	He was incredibly fickle.
Jeremiah 38:8–10	Zedekiah once again relented and told Ebed-Melech to rescue Jeremiah.	Zedekiah continually vacillated, going along with whoever was speaking at the moment.

(3a.)

Verse	Jeremiah's Words	What His Words Reveal about His Character
Jeremiah 37:6–10	Jeremiah told the king that the Babylonians would return and capture Jerusalem.	Jeremiah obediently shared God's word, even when he knew the message wouldn't be popular.
Jeremiah 37:17	Jeremiah gave Zedekiah bad news.	He always spoke God's message, even if he knew it would not be received well.
Jeremiah 38:1–4	Jeremiah continued to speak God's word even while imprisoned.	He was faithful to God no matter what the cost.

(3b.) About the only thing that Jeremiah and Zedekiah had in common was their heritage—they were both Judeans. Jeremiah was steadfastly faithful to God, never wavering, no matter what other people did to him. Zedekiah continually fluctuated between one extreme and the other. He never had his own viewpoint but went along with whoever was present at the moment. Jeremiah never showed fear, even when he knew his life was in danger on account of what he spoke. Zedekiah continually demonstrated anxiety about what would happen to him. Jeremiah always obeyed the word of the Lord. Zedekiah seemed to want to know what God said but then completely disregarded it. (4a.) Jeremiah 37:11–16: Jeremiah tried to go to the land of Benjamin. Irijah accused him of deserting to the Babylonians, then beat him and put him in a dungeon. (4b.) Jeremiah 37:21: Zedekiah rescued Jeremiah from the dungeon but still held him prisoner in the court of the guard. (4c.) Jeremiah 38:6: Jeremiah's enemies threw him into a cistern. (4d.) Jeremiah 38:10–13: Ebed-Melech rescued Jeremiah. (4e.) Jeremiah faithfully spoke God's words no matter what the cost to him personally. **Apply the Word to Your Life:** (1.) Answers will vary.

(2.) Answers will vary. (3.) Answers will vary. (4a.) God promises that opposition will not ultimately triumph because He will be with you. However, divine success may not be discernible until Judgment Day. (4b.) Answers will vary. **Create a Project:** (1.) Clay pot. (2.) "Palms Down, Palms Up Prayer." (3.) Music.

CHAPTER 5

Reflect on the Reading: Answers will vary. **Dig into the Word:** (1a.)

WORD	VERSES WHERE THIS PHRASE IS FOUND
repent, repentance	Matthew 3:2, 8, 11
baptize, Baptism	Matthew 3:6, 7, 11, 13, 14, 16

(1b.) John's whole ministry involved urging people to repent of their sins and then baptizing them after they had confessed. The act of repentance prepared their hearts—made them aware of their need for a Savior.

(2.)

VERSE	ACTION	WHAT THE ACTION REVEALS ABOUT JOHN THE BAPTIST'S CHARACTER
Matthew 3:1	John the Baptist preached in the wilderness.	He didn't seek out comfort or fame.
Matthew 3:4	John wore clothes made of camel's hair with a leather belt; he ate locusts and wild honey.	His unique lifestyle reinforced his message of repentance.
Matthew 3:6	John baptized people who confessed their sins.	He wanted to help people have a right relationship with God.

(3.)

Verse	Who John the Baptist Spoke To	What He Said	What His Words Reveal about His Character
Matthew 3:7–10	The Pharisees and Sadducees	He called them a brood of snakes (vipers) and called them to repentance. He warned them not to rely on their spiritual heritage.	John was not afraid to speak hard words even to powerful people. He lived out his mission from God.
Matthew 3:11–12	It seems he might still be talking to the Pharisees and Sadducees, but since they didn't receive Baptism from John, these words may have been spoken to the general audience.	He talked about his ministry of Baptism but also of the One coming after him. John said he was unworthy to even carry Jesus' sandals.	John was humble. He knew his mission was to point to Jesus.
Matthew 3:14	Jesus	"I need to be baptized by You; why do You come to me?"	John's humility is evident.

(4a.) Matthew 3:5–6: Crowds of people came out to the wilderness to hear John the Baptist preach and to receive his Baptism. The sheer number of people who came to him could have made him proud and caused him to forget his mission of pointing to Jesus. But we know that didn't happen. (4b.) Matthew 3:16–17: When John the Baptist baptized Jesus, he saw the heavens open and the Spirit descend like a dove. He heard a voice from heaven say, "This is My beloved Son, with whom I am well pleased." John 1:32–34 tells us that God had told John that seeing the Spirit descend and remain on a man would identify that man as the Messiah. Seeing this sight at Jesus' Baptism confirmed that Jesus was the One he had been waiting for. (5.) Answers will vary. **Apply the Word to Your Life:** (1.) They seem concerned that more people are going to Jesus than are coming to John. (2.) John doesn't seem to have the same concerns. He is happy to be the best man at the wedding and to become less so Jesus can become more. (3.) Answers will vary. (4a.) The bridesmaid or groomsman's role is to help the bridal couple enjoy their day and make the event go smoothly. They are not to upstage the bridal couple. (4b.) When we see ourselves as the supporting players instead of the stars, we can humbly glorify Jesus instead of trying to grab attention for ourselves. (5a.) Our human nature constantly wants others to notice us. We want to look better than the next person. (5b.) Answers will vary. **Create a Project:** (1.) Baptismal sign. (2.) Music.

CHAPTER 6

Reflect on the Reading: Answers will vary. **Dig into the Word:** (1a.) Answers will vary but might include the following:

WORD	VERSES WHERE THIS WORD IS FOUND
thirst, thirsty	John 4:13, 14, 15
drink	vv. 7, 9, 10, 13, 14
water	vv. 7, 10, 11, 13, 14, 15, 28
worship	vv. 20, 21, 22, 23, 24

(1b.) Jesus uses the ideas of physical thirst, drinking, and water to start a spiritual conversation with the Samaritan woman and to teach her about living water that will lead to eternal life. She brings up the topic of worship, and Jesus uses the opportunity to teach her about true worship regardless of the place. (1c.) Answers will vary. (2.)

Verse	Action	What the Action Reveals about the Samaritan Woman's Character
John 4:6–7	The Samaritan woman came to draw water in the heat of the day.	She might have been avoiding her neighbors; she might have felt shunned and rejected.
John 4:28	The woman left her water jar to go and tell her neighbors about Jesus.	She was so excited about meeting the Messiah that she completely forgot her original purpose in coming to the well.

(3a.) Her words reveal her awareness of the way the Jews view her people. They also reveal curiosity and a bit of boldness. She doesn't shy away from asking an obvious but possibly delicate question. (3b.) Now the Samaritan woman doesn't hide from her past. She uses that topic to draw her neighbors to Jesus. Again, her words display boldness. She runs to tell the people in the town. Her words also show an interest in spiritual things as she talks about the Christ (Messiah). (4a.) John 4:30: The woman's testimony immediately had an effect on her neighbors. They wanted to see the possible Messiah too. (4b.) John 4:39–42: The people believed in Jesus because of His words. But without the woman's bold witness, they would not have met Jesus. (5.) Answers will vary. **Apply the Word to Your Life:**

(1.) Jesus revealed that the woman had had five husbands and that the man she now had was not her husband. (2.) Answers will vary but might include that Jesus knew her past but still treated her with dignity and respect. He knew He would die for her too. (3.) Answers will vary. (4.) Answers will vary. (5.) Answers will vary. (6.) Answers will vary. **Create a Project:** (1.) Bookmark. (2.) Answers will vary. (3.) Music.

CHAPTER 7

Reflect on the Reading: (1.) Answers will vary. (2.) At the Last Supper, Jesus responded to the disciples' quarrel over who was greatest: "And He said to them, 'The kings of the Gentiles exercise lordship over them, and those in authority over them are called benefactors. But not so with you. Rather, let the greatest among you become as the youngest, and the leader as one who serves'" (Luke 22:25–26). In God's kingdom, greatness comes through service. (3.) Answers will vary. (4.) Answers will vary. **Dig into the Word:** (1a.)

VERSES	KEY WORDS FOUND IN THESE VERSES
Matthew 26:70, 72, 75	denied, deny
Matthew 26:70, 72, 74	know

(1b.) Peter's biggest failure was in denying his Savior and Lord. Peter knew Jesus better than most people because he spent three years with Him. But he denied that knowledge because of fear. (2.) Answers will vary but might include the following:

Gospel	Mark 14:66–72	Matthew 26:69–75	Luke 22:54–62	John 18:15–18, 25–27
Peter's Actions	Peter warmed himself by the fire in the court-yard. He denied knowing Jesus to two servant girls and another bystander. When the rooster crowed, Peter remembered Jesus' words. Peter wept.	Matthew includes that when Peter denied Jesus the second time, he was standing by the entrance of the court-yard.	Luke includes that Peter followed Jesus at a distance. He tells that an hour passed between the second and third denials. He writes that Peter saw Jesus looking at him when the rooster crowed.	John adds that another disciple—probably John himself—was with Peter in the courtyard and that it was John who was able to get them both inside. He also adds that the third accuser was a relative of the man whose ear Peter had cut off.

(3a.) Answers will vary, but might include the following:

Verse	What Peter Said	How His Words Escalated
Matthew 26:70	"I don't know what you mean."	At first, Peter only said he didn't know what the servant girl meant. He didn't say that he didn't know Jesus.
Matthew 26:72	"I do not know the man."	This time, Peter said that he didn't know the man, didn't know Jesus. He also denied it with an oath.
Matthew 26:74	"I do not know the man."	He called down a curse upon himself if he wasn't telling the truth.

(3b.) Since Peter had lived and worked with Jesus for about three years, he certainly recognized Jesus. He probably knew a lot about Jesus' personality and ways of doing things. (3c.) At the point of denial, it seems Peter did not cherish Jesus and had more fear for his own safety than regard for his friend. In one sense, Peter probably did not understand Jesus at all because he had an incorrect view of what *Messiah* meant. (4a.) Luke includes the important detail of Jesus looking at Peter (Luke 22:61–62). (4b.) Answers will vary. **Apply the Word to Your Life:** (1a.) Jesus prayed for Peter because Satan had asked permission to test the disciples and Jesus knew Peter would deny Him. (1b.) Jesus prayed Peter's faith would not fail completely but that Peter would return and use the experience to strengthen others. (1c.) Answers will vary. (2a.) Jesus told Peter to pray that he wouldn't give in to temptation. (2b.) Peter—and all of us—need to pray this prayer because even though our hearts may want to follow Jesus, our sinful self is weak and often gives in to Satan's lures. (2c.) Answers will vary. **Create a Project:** (1.) Answers will vary. (2.) Music.

CHAPTER 8

Reflect on the Reading: Answers will vary. **Dig into the Word:** (1a.) Answers will vary but might include the following:

WORD OR PHRASE	VERSES WHERE THESE APPEAR
see, seeing, seen, sight, vision	Acts 9:7, 8, 9, 10, 12, 17, 18
threats, murder, persecuting, suffer	vv. 1, 4, 5, 16
name	vv. 10, 11, 12, 14, 15, 16, 21

(1b.) Possible themes include physical and spiritual vision; Saul persecuting and Paul suffering; a name represents character and reputation. (1c.) These themes are important because once Saul's physical vision was restored, the Holy Spirit gave him true spiritual vision. Saul spent his early life persecuting the Church, but Paul was often tortured and beaten for his faith in Jesus. Saul later changed his name to Paul, perhaps indicating his radical transformation. Saul persecuted those who called on the name of Jesus, but he became God's instrument to carry His name to the Gentiles.

(2.)

Verses	Action	What the Action Reveals about Saul's Character
Before meeting Jesus Acts 9:1–2	Breathing murderous threats, going to high priest for permission to arrest believers in Jesus	Zealous for Judaism, determined to stamp out what he saw as a false religion
After meeting Jesus but before regaining sight Acts 9:3–17	Fell to the ground, heard Jesus speaking, was led into Damascus, didn't eat or drink for three days	Exhibited humility and contrition
After regaining his sight Acts 9:18–25	Rose, was baptized, ate and drank, proclaimed Jesus as the Son of God, escaped Damascus in a basket	Total transformation

(3a.) Paul says, "Who are You, Lord?" An interesting question since in Philippians 3:8 Paul says, "I count everything as loss because of the surpassing worth of knowing Christ Jesus my Lord." (3b.) For the rest of his life, Paul's character was defined by joyfully discovering the answer to that question. (4a.) The narrator reveals Paul's zeal both before and after meeting Jesus. Before meeting Jesus, he persecuted people following Christ; after meeting Jesus, he couldn't stop talking about Him. (4b.) The narrator shows Ananias's obedience. He questions the wisdom of going to Saul but does it anyway. (4c.) The narrator shows both the skepticism of the Damascus disciples when Saul first began preaching Jesus and also their willingness to protect him when he had proven himself genuine. (4d.) The narrator reveals the willingness of the Jews in Damascus to kill to protect their faith. **Apply the Word to Your Life:** Answers will vary. **Create a Project:** (1.) Answers will vary. (2.) Music.

ENDNOTES

1. John H. Walton, *Genesis*, The NIV Application Commentary, accessed September 13, 2021, www.bible gateway.com/passage/?search =Genesis+39&version=NIV &resource_entry=nivac-genesis /from-slave-to-prisoner-39-1 -23&tab=study.

2. *NKJV Cultural Backgrounds Study Bible: Bringing to Life the Ancient World of Scripture* (Grand Rapids, MI: Zondervan, 2017), Kindle.

3. Walton, *Genesis*, The NIV Application Commentary (Grand Rapids, MI: Zondervan, 2001), accessed September 13, 2021, www.biblegateway .com/passage/?search=Genesis +39&version=NIV&resource_entry =nivac-genesis/genesis-37-1-47 -26&tab=study.

4. Robert Alter, *The Art of Biblical Narrative* (New York: Basic Books, 2011), Kindle.

5. *NIV Archaeological Study Bible: An Illustrated Walk Through Biblical History and Culture* (Grand Rapids, MI: Zondervan, 2005), 67.

6. *NKJV Cultural Backgrounds Study Bible*, Kindle.

7. Blue Letter Bible, accessed September 14, 2021, www.blueletterbible.org /lexicon/h6743/kjv/wlc/0-1/.

8. William D. Mounce, *Mounce's Complete Expository Dictionary of Old and New Testament Words* (Grand Rapids, MI: Zondervan, 2006), accessed on Accordance Version XII Bible software "PROSPER," MED, 547. https:// accordance.bible/link/read /Mounce_Expository#8622.

9. Kenneth L. Barker and John R. Kohlenberger III, *The Expositor's Bible Commentary, Abridged Edition: Old Testament* (Grand Rapids, MI: Zondervan, Harper Collins Publishers, 1994), accessed September 13, 2021, www.biblegateway.com /passage/?search=Genesis+39 &version=NIV&resource_entry=ebc -abridged-ot/ge-39-7-20&tab=study.

10. Warren W. Wiersbe, *Genesis 25–50, Be Authentic: Exhibiting Real Faith in a Real World*, The BE Series (Colorado Springs: David C. Cook, 1997), accessed September 13, 2021, www .biblegateway.com/passage /?search=Genesis+39&version =NIV&resource_entry =wiersbe-be-bible-study /learning-wait-39-21-23&tab=study.

11. Barker and Kohlenberger, *The Expositor's Bible Commentary*, accessed September 13, 2021, www.biblegateway .com/passage/?search =Joshua+2&version=ESV &resource_entry=ebc-abridged-ot /jos-2-2-3&tab=study.

12. *NIV Archaeological Study Bible*, 312.

13. *NIV Archaeological Study Bible*, 306.

14. *The Lutheran Study Bible*, 343.

15. *NIV Archaeological Study Bible*, 305.

16. I first told this story at www .incourage.me/2017/06 /surprising-gift-saying-yes .html?utm_source=Sailthru&utm _medium=email&utm_campaign =%28in%29courage+Daily +Devotion+2017-06-14&utm _term=%28in%29courage +Daily+Devotion, October 6, 2021.

17. Paul E. Kretzmann, *Popular Commentary of the Bible: The Old Testament*, vol. 1 (St. Louis: Concordia Publishing House, 1921), 371.

18. Kretzmann, *Popular Commentary of the Bible: The Old Testament*, vol. 1, 372.

19. *The Lutheran Study Bible*, 343.

20. Eugene H. Peterson, *Leap Over a Wall: Earthy Spirituality for Everyday Christians* (New York: Harper One, 1997), 3.

21   John R. Mittelstaedt, *1 and 2 Samuel,* People's Bible Commentary (St. Louis: Concordia Publishing House, 1995, 2005), 186.

22   Mittelstaedt, *1 and 2 Samuel,* People's Bible Commentary, 232.

23   *Lutheran Bible Companion,* vol. 1 (St. Louis: Concordia Publishing House, 2014), 294.

24   Peterson, *Leap Over a Wall,* 160.

25   Mittelstaedt, *1 and 2 Samuel,* People's Bible Commentary, 325.

26   Mittelstaedt, *1 and 2 Samuel,* People's Bible Commentary, 90.

27   *Lutheran Bible Companion,* vol. 1, 300.

28   *The Lutheran Study Bible,* 1203.

29   *NIV Archaeological Study Bible,* 1259.

30   *Life Application Bible: New International Version* (Wheaton, IL: Tyndale House Publishers Inc. and Grand Rapids, MI: Zondervan Publishing House, 1988, 1989, 1990, 1991), 1288.

31   John Arthur Nunes, *Meant for More: In, With, and Under the Ordinary* (St. Louis: Concordia Publishing House, 2020), Kindle.

32   *The Lutheran Study Bible,* 842.

33   *The Lutheran Study Bible,* 1250.

34   Eugene H. Peterson, *Run with the Horses: The Quest for Life at Its Best* (Downers Grove, IL: Intervarsity-Press, 1983, 2009), Kindle.

35   Mounce, *Mounce's Complete Expository Dictionary of Old and New Testament Words,* accessed on Accordance XII Bible software "PROSPER," MED, 547. https://accordance.bible/link/read/Mounce_Expository#8622.

36   *The Lutheran Study Bible,* 1708.

37   Michael J. Wilkins, *Matthew,* The NIV Application Commentary (Grand Rapids, MI: Zondervan, 2004), accessed September 16, 2021, www.biblegateway.com/passage/?search=Matthew%203&version=ESV&resource_entry=nivac-matthew/john-the-baptist-prepares-the-way-3-1-6&tab=study.

38   Kretzmann, *The Popular Commentary of the Bible: New Testament,* vol. 1, 165.

39   *The Lutheran Study Bible,* 1655.

40   *The Lutheran Study Bible,* 1655.

41   Gary P. Baumler, *John,* People's Bible Commentary (St. Louis: Concordia Publishing House, 1997, 2005), 26.

42   *The Lutheran Study Bible,* 1582.

43   David E. Garland, *Mark,* The NIV Application Commentary (Grand Rapids, MI: Zondervan, 1996), accessed September 16, 2021, www.biblegateway.com/passage/?search=Mark+6&version=ESV&resource_entry=nivac-mark/the-death-of-john-the-baptizer-6-14-29&tab=study.

44   *The Lutheran Study Bible,* 1667.

45   Kretzmann, *The Popular Commentary of the Bible: New Testament,* vol. 1, 61.

46   Wilkins, *Matthew,* The NIV Application Commentary, accessed September 16, 2021, www.biblegateway.com/passage/?search=matthew+11&version=ESV&resource_entry=nivac-matthew/john-the-baptist-questions-jesus-11-1-6&tab=study.

47   Kretzmann, *The Popular Commentary of the Bible: New Testament,* vol. 1, 425.

48   Wilkins, *Matthew,* The NIV Application Commentary, accessed September 29, 2021, www.biblegateway.com/passage/?search=Matthew+3&version=ESV&resource_entry=nivac-matthew/john-the-baptist-prepares-the-way-3-1-6&tab=study.

49   *Life Application Bible: New International Version,* 1871.

50   Baumler, *John,* People's Bible Commentary, 60.

51   *The Lutheran Study Bible,* 1557.

52 Gary M. Burge, *John*, The NIV Application Commentary (Grand Rapids, MI: Zondervan, 2000), accessed September 29, 2021, www.biblegateway.com/passage/?search=John+4&version=ESV&resource_entry=nivac-john/jesus-and-the-samaritan-woman-4-1-26&tab=study.

53 *Archaeological Study Bible*, 1727.

54 *Archaeological Study Bible*, 1737.

55 *Everyday Matters Bible for Women: New Living Translation* (Peabody, MA: Hendrickson Publishers Marketing, LLC, 2012), 1272.

56 Burge, *John*, The NIV Application Commentary, accessed September 29, 2021, www.biblegateway.com/passage/?search=John+4&version=ESV&resource_entry=nivac-john/jesus-and-the-samaritan-woman-4-1-26&tab=study.

57 Baumler, *John*, People's Bible Commentary, 69.

58 Warren W. Wiersbe, *The Gospels*, The BE Series (Colorado Springs: David C. Cook, 2015), Kindle.

59 *The Lutheran Study Bible*, 1786.

60 *The Lutheran Study Bible*, 1786.

61 Baumler, *John*, People's Bible Commentary, 64.

62 Kretzmann, *Popular Commentary of the Bible: New Testament*, vol. 1, 430.

63 "Deaconess Ministry," August 2, 2021, www.lcms.org/how-we-serve/mercy/deaconess-ministry.

64 Baumler, *John*, People's Bible Commentary, 66.

65 *Archaeological Study Bible*, 1726.

66 Michael Card, *A Fragile Stone: The Emotional Life of Simon Peter* (Downer's Grove, IL: InterVarsity Press, 2003), Kindle.

67 Wilkins, *Matthew*, The NIV Application Commentary, accessed September 29, 2021, www.biblegateway.com/passage/?search=Matthew+16&version=ESV&resource_entry=nivac-matthew/jesus-messiah-predicts-his-suffering-and-resurrection-16-21-23&tab=study.

68 Wilkins, *Matthew*, The NIV Application Commentary, accessed September 29, 2021, www.biblegateway.com/passage/?search=Matthew+26&version=ESV&resource_entry=nivac-matthew/peters-denials-of-jesus-26-69-75&tab=study.

69 *NKJV Cultural Backgrounds Study Bible*, Kindle.

70 Mounce, *Mounce's Complete Expository Dictionary of Old and New Testament Words*, accessed September 29, 2021, www.biblegateway.com/passage/?search=Luke+22&version=ESV&resource_entry=mounce-expository-dictionary/look-1&tab=study.

71 *The Lutheran Study Bible*, 1767.

72 Baumler, *John*, People's Bible Commentary, 272.

73 Baumler, *John*, People's Bible Commentary, 271–72.

74 Card, *A Fragile Stone*, Kindle.

75 *The Lutheran Study Bible*, 1765.

76 *Luther's Small Catechism with Explanation* (St. Louis: Concordia Publishing House, 2017), 269.

77 Scholars say that "stretch out your hands" indicated crucifixion.

78 Paul David Tripp, *New Morning Mercies: A Daily Gospel Devotional* (Wheaton, IL: Crossway, 2014), Kindle.

79 Charles R. Swindoll, *Paul: A Man of Grace and Grit* (Nashville: The W Publishing Group, 2002), 5.

80 R. C. H. Lenski, *The Interpretation of St. Paul's Epistles to the Galatians, Ephesians and Philippians* (Minneapolis, MN: Augsburg Publishing House, 1937, 1946, 1961), 833.

81 R. C. H. Lenski, *The Interpretation of I and II Corinthians* (Minneapolis, MN: Augsburg Publishing House, 1937, 1963), 1268–69.

82 Swindoll, *Paul: A Man of Grace and Grit*, 6.

83 *The Lutheran Study Bible*, 1557.

84 R. C. H. Lenski, *The Interpretation of The Acts of the Apostles* (Minneapolis, MN: Augsburg Publishing House, 1934, 1944, 1961), 314.

85 "The Rules of the Pharisees," accessed July 28, 2021, www.pursuegod.org /rules-pharisees/.

86 "Sabbath," accessed July 28, 2021, www.bibleask.org/rules -pharisees-made-sabbath -observance/.

87 Commentators think this Arabia refers to the Nebataean Kingdom in the area around Damascus. *The Lutheran Study Bible*, 2003.

88 Blue Letter Bible, accessed September 28, 2021, www.blueletterbible.org /lexicon/g3972/kjv/tr/0-1/.

89 Lenski, *The Interpretation of I and II Corinthians*, 1302.

90 Team Hoyt, accessed September 29, 2021, www.teamhoytcda.com /the-story-of-team-hoyt/.

91 Lenski, *The Interpretation of I and II Corinthians*, 1305.

92 Lenski, *The Interpretation of St. Paul's Epistles to the Galatians, Ephesians and Philippians*, 837.

93 Tripp, *New Morning Mercies*, Kindle.

94 Alter, *The Art of Biblical Narrative*, Kindle.

95 Alter, *The Art of Biblical Narrative*, Kindle.

96 Alter, *The Art of Biblical Narrative*, Kindle.

97 Alter, *The Art of Biblical Narrative*, Kindle.

98 *NIV Biblical Theology Study Bible* (Grand Rapids, MI: Zondervan, 2018), accessed September 29, 2021, www.biblegateway.com/passage /?search=Joshua+2&version=ESV &resource_entry=niv-biblical -theology/jos-2-9-11&tab=study.

99 *Luther's Small Catechism with Explanation*, 292.

100 Prayer on sign taken from *Luther's Small Catechism with Explanation*, 291.

101 Blue Letter Bible, accessed July 2, 2021, www.blueletterbible.org /lexicon/g1492/kjv/tr/0-1/.

102 Sharla Fritz, *Soul Spa: 40 Days of Spiritual Renewal* (St. Louis: Concordia Publishing House, 2015), 48.

NOTES